THE FOLLOWING STATEMENT IS FROM JOSEPH SCHULL, RCNVR OFFICER, 1941-45, AND AUTHOR OF *THE FAR DISTANT SHIPS*, THE OFFICIAL ACCOUNT OF CANADIAN SECOND WORLD WAR NAVAL OPERATIONS:

"I don't know Jim Lamb, but I wish I did. I think his book is superb. For me, and I'm sure for anyone who had anything to do with the navy, the whole thing comes alive again, just as it really was. In its humor, its understanding, its vivid descriptions, its general warmth and realness, the book encompasses the whole of those years—and not only for the men who lived through them. It's good enough and lively enough to be enjoyed by anyone, whether or not he's ever seen a ship. Besides that, as a segment of the country's history, told in terms of people, it's a gem."

THE CORVETTE NAVY

the way it really was in World War II— as it should always be remembered.

"A grand book . . . brings alive the horror and humor of Canada's war at sea."
—OTTAWA CITIZEN

"Vivid and fresh descriptions of strife and circumstances at sea." —BOOKS IN CANADA

"A fine book, with some truly magnificent moments . . . exciting and enriching!"
—HALIFAX LOYALIST

Nonfiction Bestsellers from SIGNET

THE
CORVETTE
NAVY

~~~~~~

True Stories from
Canada's Atlantic War

James B. Lamb

A SIGNET BOOK
Published by
Macmillan—NAL Publishing Limited
Scarborough, Ontario

PUBLISHED BY
THE NEW AMERICAN LIBRARY
OF CANADA LIMITED

This is an authorized reprint of a hardcover edition published by
Macmillan Company of Canada Ltd.

First Signet Printing, February, 1979

1   2   3   4   5   6   7   8   9

PRINTED IN CANADA

COVER PRINTED IN U.S.A.

DEDICATION

~~~~~~~~~~~~~~~~~~~~~~~~~~~~~~

The little ships of the corvette navy have
vanished from the oceans of the world, as
quickly and quietly as they came. They
live today only in a few fading
photographs, and in the memories of
middle-aged men scattered across the
breadth of Canada who once sailed them
through the winter gales of the wartime
North Atlantic.

To these men, and especially to the Naval
Reserve officers from the merchant
service who taught and led them, this
book is respectfully dedicated.

AUTHOR'S NOTE

To the best of my memory, all the
incidents related in this book are true.
The chapter "Slip and Proceed" describes
a typical escort group sailing, rather than
a particular convoy; the convoy number
used is fictitious.

CONTENTS

~~~~~~~~~~~~~~~~~~

1
THE LAST CORVETTE

~~~~~~

As these words are written, a small steel steamship lies deserted in a corner of the dockyard at Halifax, her work done, her future uncertain. Years of toil as a tender to an oceanic research institute have altered her silhouette, replacing guns with winches and adding excrescences of various kinds, but there is no mistaking that raked, circular-sectioned funnel in its cluster of ventilators, that jaunty duck's-bottom stern or that long, flaring fo'c'sle. Her origins have been long forgotten on today's busy waterfront, but this work-worn little drudge is the last survivor of one of history's proudest fleets, the last Canadian example of a Second World War creation as famous and successful as the Spitfire or the jeep.

This ship was once His Majesty's Canadian Ship *Sackville*, and for all her obscurity and neglect she is as significant a survival to the people of Canada as HMS *Victory* is to the British or USS *Constitution* to the United States. For she is a corvette, the largest and most successful class of escort warship ever built, and she and her sisters once made Canada one of the major naval powers of the world. More than that: this little ship, and all the others like her, were the principal weapon which brought victory in the war's longest, bitterest, and most vital battle, and thus assured the survival of the free world.

It is appropriate that this last vessel should have lingered in a Canadian wartime port, for the corvette played a greater part in the growth and character of the Canadian navy than it did in any other naval force, and its influence can be seen in the Canadian naval service to this day. More than any other ship, weapon, or aircraft, the corvette had a distinctively Canadian connotation, her limitations and capabilities reflecting to a remarkable degree those of a new and growing Canadian navy, so that she came almost to reflect the character of the men who sailed in her. For both corvettes and their crews were to blossom like so many Cinderellas; from humble origins, despised by the professional crews of regular naval ships, they were destined to become the belles of the ball, the backbone of the victorious Atlantic escort fleet, and the developers of a tradition and an expertise uniquely their own, which was to be the envy of their regular-navy sisters.

The corvette was born of the Munich crisis of 1938, which convinced the board of the British Admiralty that war with Germany was inevitable and imminent. The Royal Navy began at once to gear itself for war by 1940, and its first requirement was for escorts to protect the huge and vulnerable overseas trade carried in British ships to every corner of the world. Existing types of warships were far too elaborate for quick production; hundreds of escorts were needed which could be built and ready in a year's time. As it had in the First World War, the Admiralty turned to the well-known Middlesbrough shipbuilders, Smith's Dock Company, for a design suitable for emergency production, and again this famous firm came through with an effective solution.

The design it proposed, and the Admiralty accepted, was based on the lines of a recently built whale-catching vessel called *Southern Pride*, but with more powerful engines and consequently greater speed. She was to be of approximately 1200 tons displacement with an overall length of 205 feet, a beam of 33 feet, and a draught of 15 feet. Driven by a single three-bladed propeller, she was to have a maximum speed of 16 knots and a really remarkable endurance of 4000 miles at 12 knots on only 200 tons of oil fuel. Her machinery—four-cylinder triple-expansion reciprocating engines of 2750 horsepower, and twin cylindrical Scotch boilers—was deliberately kept simple, for ease both of manufacture and of operation, and the whole design was intended from the beginning to be capable of production by every sort of engineering firm other than the big shipbuilders, which were now crammed to capacity with large warship orders.

Main armament of the new escorts was to be the depth-charge, discharged both from traps in the stern and by mortars—"throwers"—in the waist, with a surface armament of a single four-inch gun and a two-pounder pom-pom, backed up by machine guns, for anti-aircraft protection. Named "corvette", the French word for "sloop", the new escort with its modest 47-man complement was intended only as a stop-gap until something better could be provided.

But all unrecognized in these plans was a touch of genius; the dowdy maid-of-all-work had been endowed by her Good Fairy with a wholly unexpected range of qualities. For this ship of humble design proved to be capable of amazing versatility, able to carry more than twice her designed complement and a seemingly endless accumulation of ever more sophisticated armament and instrumentation. She could keep the sea in weather that overwhelmed huge merchant vessels and reduced destroyers to water-logged hulks; she could be used for anything from minesweeping to anti-aircraft protection. But, greatest blessing of all, she could turn on a dime, the only Allied warship with a turning circle tighter than that of a submarine, and in consequence she was the master of the U-boat in manoeuvring duels that would foil any other surface escort.

Adaptable and flexible in an ever-changing war, the corvette became the backbone of the Allied escort force, going through endless modifications and improvements in the course of the building of no fewer than 269 ships, the largest warship class ever built.

Ultimately she evolved into a new class; two sets of corvette engines were jammed into a lengthened corvette hull to gain a little more speed, and the resulting super-corvette was called a "frigate". By the war's end, frigates and corvettes made up almost the entire strength of the Allied escort forces in the Atlantic, and their crews of reservists had brought the techniques of convoy escort and submarine detection and destruction to new heights of expertise. But they had also founded a tradition of colourful character and eccentric individualism a world away from the stereotype of the professional serviceman; a tradition cherished to this day in moments of nostalgia by middle-aged men in cities and towns across Canada.

Right from the beginning, there was something suspect about corvettes in the eyes of right-thinking professional navy men; what was one to make of a man-of-war that looked like a fish trawler and called itself HMS *Pansy*? For the Admiralty, in a moment of inspiration, had designated the new ships as the Flower class, a tradition in escort vessels begun in the First World War. Each Royal Navy corvette was named after a flower, and the world was enriched by sea-stained fighting ships glorying in the name of His Majesty's Ship *Pennywort*, *Crocus*, or *Tulip*. There was a *Convolvulus*, a *Saxifrage*, and a *Cowslip*. But even a Board of Admiralty has a heart; eventually, HMS *Pansy* was allowed a change of name by a repentant Ships' Names Committee. She became HMS *Heartsease*.

By the time the Royal Navy had built more than a hundred corvettes, flower names were becoming difficult to come by; HMS *Bulrush* probably reflects the growing desperation of this latter period, while HMS *Burdock* and HMS *Ling* show just how far the naming committee was prepared to cast its net. In Canada, HMCS *Poison Ivy* was openly conceded to be a possibility, but cooler heads prevailed; the Canadians decided to name their corvettes after towns and villages, although a handful of flower names—*Spikenard*, *Snowberry*, *Windflower*, etc.—were incorporated with ships originally built for the Royal Navy but taken over by the RCN.

It was widely believed in the wartime Allied navies that the naming of the Flower class was part of a form of psychological warfare practised on the enemy by a vengeful Britain; there must be an added ignoming, it was felt, to being sunk by HMS *Poppy*, as U605 was, or to bring outfought and captured by a fierce HMS *Hyacinth*, as was the Italian submarine *Peria*. It was one thing to perish in the Wagnerian splendour hankered after by Hitler, but quite another for the proud Teuton to be vanquished by *Rhododendron*, as U104 was, or sunk by *Periwinkle*, like U147.

From the beginning, there was something faintly comic about corvettes, and it was an element which their own crews were to cherish and embellish as part of their jealously preserved attitude of enlightened amateurism in a world of professional inanity. The name of their ship was, for the stockbrokers and students, clerks and farmers who manned *Violet* and *Gladiolus* and *Marigold*, a snook cocked at the whole professional establishment, and in particular at the vainglorious German U-boats with their brass bands and "We are sailing against England" nonsense. There was nothing fancy about corvettes, either in their names or in their crews, and this was just the way corvette men chose to have it.

Although Canadian crews were spared the blushes of those who manned HMS *Pink* or HMS *Wallflower*, they had a few names of their own which were considered a little peculiar. Nobody thought much of HMCS *Asbestos* as a name for a fighting ship, while HMCS *Norsyd* and HMCS *Stonetown* raised a few eyebrows in the escort ports. But by and large, corvette types took pride, however perverse, in the name of their ship, and did their best to associate it with the ship's crest, usually painted on the gunshield of the forward four-inch. These designs, though they would have been the despair of the Royal College of Heralds, were nonetheless lively, if not downright lurid; it would be hard to conceive anything more apt than the five aces displayed as the crest of HMCS *Baddeck*, or more vivid than the crowned lady falling on her backside into a puddle on the gunshield of HMCS *Wetaskiwin* (Wet-ass-Queen).

Whether named for flower or village, the corvettes, and later those super-corvettes, the frigates, were churned out in dozens by shipyards and engineering firms in Canada, some of whom had never before built a ship. More than 130 corvettes and half a hundred frigates were built in this country alone, and the British built even more, including ships for the Free French and United States navies. The trickle of new corvettes began in Britain in 1940, and in Canada by the spring of 1941; within a year it had become a flood of fat-funnelled, jaunty little ships. They grew to become a force that ruled the Atlantic; the seas were covered with them, and they clustered thick about the quays and trot-buoys in every naval port in the northern hemisphere.

Today they have disappeared as if they had never been; they survive only in the memories of aging men, and in this single forgotten veteran in a dockyard backwater. This is the story of that vanished fleet of ships, and of the colourful crews who sailed them across a wartime North Atlantic.

2
THE TWO NAVIES

~~~~~~

Canada had two navies in the Second World War. First, of course, was the Royal Canadian Navy, the big navy, the "real" navy, the "pusser" navy. It was, as its corps of public relations officers endlessly reiterated, a very big deal indeed. Thousands upon thousands of uniformed men and women filled teeming offices and training establishments, vast and ever-growing complexes of brick and concrete, representing the investment of hundreds of millions of dollars. Its organization, embracing dozens of commands, hundreds of departments, and thousands of experts and specialists, ranging from physicists to dietitians, from jurists to journalists, was a triumph of administrative genius which represented one of the nation's major wartime accomplishments.

It is fashionable in peacetime to deride the capacity of service bureaucrats, but not even General Motors or any other of the civilian corporate giants has ever managed, in time of peace, anything to compare with the administrative miracle of the wartime RCN, which grew from eighteen hundred officers and men into a vast and complex machine of almost a hundred thousand men and women.

Here was the repository of naval tradition, the showcase of talent and ability, the dynamic centre of thrust and growth and expansion. Vast though it was by mid-war, it yet thrived and grew in every direction as busy men were driven to seek more assistants, more space in which to operate. Here was pay and pace and promotion, here was where it was all at.

Each morning, at parade grounds across the country, on prairie and seacoast, scores of white ensigns ascended proudly into the clear Canadian air; bands played and gunner's mates shouted and thousands of feet marched in unison. Dozens of gym floors and paved parking lots earned the respectful salute traditionally accorded the quarterdeck, the abode of authority. In Ottawa and Halifax, and indeed in every city throughout the land, hundreds of uniformed naval officers dumped their briefcases in hundreds of office cubicles, eased themselves behind their desks, and opened their morning newspapers to begin yet another day.

A vast fleet of vessels of every sort was attached to this great navy; literally hundreds of coastal mortar launches, harbour craft, and training vessels, armed yachts and gate ships, harbour minesweepers and picket boats; all the endless numbers and variety of the "9 to 5" fleet.

But the real strength of the Big Navy lay ashore. Its admirals flew their flags from office buildings, and its officers and men, ratings and Wrens, had their wardrooms and messdecks in shore establishments, land-bound battleships these, bearing old and famous naval names.

It was a tremendous force, embodying some of the best brains in the country and involving a significant proportion of the nation's wealth and manpower. Although manned by reservists in their thousands, it was directed by professional naval officers, and its operations were oriented to a hierarchy which included every senior officer the country possessed, or could borrow from abroad. What it all accomplished would be difficult to define, but of necessity it was preoccupied with recruiting, training, housing, feeding, administering, and caring for itself, a great and endless task.

Canada's second navy was a much different force: a bunch of amateur sailors, recruited from every walk of civilian life, manning ships deemed too small for command by professional naval officers. The ships—Algerines, corvettes, frigates, Bangors—were as cheap as they could be built, and their officers and men were involved, not with admirals and captains, but with characters like Two-Gun Ryan, Harry the Horse, Death Ray, Foghorn Davis, and The Mad Spaniard. It was an amateur, improvised, cut-rate navy, but its purpose and accomplishment were clear: it fought, and won, the Battle of the Atlantic. This was the corvette navy, the little navy, Canada's other navy, manned by amateurs like me.

The division between the two navies was surprisingly complete and clear-cut; few regular career Canadian naval officers ever kept watch aboard a corvette, and only a handful of corvette crewmen were RCN ratings. For shortly after the outbreak of war, a strange process began. The little handful of professional naval officers—all that the country possessed and the only Canadians trained over long peacetime years to fight a war at sea—were bustled ashore into offices. There they presided over clerks and typists in a series of administrative posts for which they had received no training at all. Most of them never went to sea again.

Their places afloat were taken by a handful of former merchant seamen, now officers of the Royal Canadian Reserve, and by young men in the Royal Canadian Naval Volunteer Reserve, many of whom were culled from offices ashore and most of whom had never been to sea before. It was a situation worthy of Gilbert and Sullivan: trained seamen were put in offices ashore and trained office managers were sent to sea. As a result, Canada's professional naval officers were to play an ever-diminishing role in the Battle of the Atlantic.

This curious situation had been brought about by a miscalculation of the role the corvettes could play in the naval war. Originally they had been regarded as a stop-gap, and, as such, unworthy as commands for Canada's few, and precious, trained naval officers. Apart from those allowed afloat in the RCN's handful of pre-war destroyers, permanent-force officers were hoarded ashore against the time when the new superships would appear to fight the glorious Armageddon against Germany's powerful surface fleet. Meanwhile, the little jerry-built corvettes were filled up with reservists and packed off to do what they could in the squalid brawls with U-boats around the herds of merchantmen. While waiting ashore, RCN officers accumulated experience in positions of responsibility, and the promotions that went with them; a few years ashore could do more for a fellow than a lifetime afloat.

But a funny thing happened to the regular navy while it waited for the Big Ships that were to fight the Big Battle. For as the years wore on, it became clear that the little battle, the U-boat thing, was in fact the Big Battle after all, and the little ships that were fighting it were all that were going to matter. The RCN pursued its original "big ship" notions to the very end: after weary years of construction that had earned them the names of *Moses* and *Methuselah*, the two Tribal-class destroyers that had been building in the Halifax shipyards since before living memory were finally commissioned and in the closing years of the war joined their British-built sisters in operations with the British Home Fleet; and as the German war ended, the RCN took over two British cruisers. Canada's Tribals covered themselves with glory, particularly in Channel shoot-ups along the invasion coasts, but for all that, their operations, however exciting were a sideshow. The main event was fought out, month after exhausting month, in the North Atlantic. For the issue was, simply, command of the sea; whoever held it held the initiative, and could fight where, when, and how he chose.

The Germans picked the U-boat as their weapon in the duel for ocean supremacy, and consequently it was the anti-submarine forces of the Allies, not their battle fleets, which were principally involved. Thus, it was the little work-worn corvettes, frigates, and over-age destroyers of the escort groups which contributed most to the Allied victory, rather than their more glamorous and heavily gunned RCN sisters.

From the very beginning, the men of the little navy were left largely on their own. A bewildered RCNR lieutenant, only a month or two away from his second mate's berth in some merchant ship, his two interwoven curly strips of gold lace still bright on each cuff, was dumped off at a shipbuilding yard to take over his new corvette command, with three or four officers as green to the navy as himself and sixty or seventy young men fresh from the prairies or city pavements who had never seen the sea before. If the new captain was lucky, one of his officers might have some practical experience of pilotage or navigation, if not too seasick to care. If his chief engineer had worked in a locomotive roundhouse and knew a little about steam engines, the captain felt himself to be fortunate indeed.

In the ensuing purgatory, the corvette captain learned to depend chiefly on his own resources, with help and advice from his fellow corvette commanders or, if he was lucky enough to have a good one, from his group senior officer, who in the early days of the war was usually a professional naval officer commanding a destroyer, either RN or RCN. Certainly he got no help from the shore establishment, not even from those officers who were supposedly responsible for the administration of his ship; I was myself commissioned into one of the early corvettes, and in all the subsequent years at sea we were never visited by any of the Canadian Captains Destroyers, or "Captains D", as they were called, whose direct responsibility we were, or for that matter, by any officer above the rank of commander.

Ah, yes; there was that one occasion . . .

During the preparations for the invasion of Europe, a

flotilla of Canadian fleet minesweepers lay off Spithead working up for the assault on Normandy, where they were to precede the landing craft carrying the first wave of troops. It was an exciting place at an exciting time; the Channel ports were jammed with shipping and Britain was crammed with troops, all trained and keyed-up to the highest pitch for what everyone knew was to be the turning point of the whole war. There was a sense of occasion abroad; all about us were the preparations for the greatest combined operation ever attempted by man, and here, at first hand, were the great leaders of the free world.

From our vantage-point alongside a dock wall, we had seen our king, George VI, and felt our hearts surge as the slim figure in naval uniform drove past us. From the beginning we had "fought for George"; now here he was, in person, and we stared, with awkward reverence, at the earnest, dedicated man whose faith and purpose had so inspired us in far-off Canada. Churchill came next, with his jaunty wave and jutting cigar, and in the days that followed we saw a succession of the great commanders who were to lead us. There was the hawk-faced Admiral Vian of the Royal Navy, an unsmiling Admiral Kirk of the United States Navy, and then the familiar Monty, in his black beret with all the badges, leaning out of an open car as he toured his cheering troops. From the ships we caught only a glimpse of Eisenhower, but like everyone else we were fiercely proud to be led by Ike, who, more than any other leader, awoke instant affection, loyalty, and respect in the servicemen of every country.

But in all this parade of Allied personalities, Canada felt itself to be missing the boat; her servicemen abroad were being seduced by the glamour of foreign, if Allied, powers. The word went out to London and we received, at last, our first and only visit by a representative of the Real Canadian Navy. Vice-Admiral Percy Nelles, a nice little man who looked a bit like radio comedian Ed Wynn and who had spent the greater part of his wartime career in Ottawa, came down from London to visit us. We followed him dutifully as he trotted about our immaculate decks and inspected our paraded crew, and then saw him piped over the side back to his waiting car. A short, plump little man with very thick glasses, he was not exactly a warrior leader calculated to fire our blood on the eve of this great assault, but he represented a Canadian presence in the big-brass department; Ottawa had countered Washington and London admiral for admiral. In the battle of the big guns, Vice-Admiral Percy Nelles rated as Canada's Answer.

The occasion, however, was unique; in all the long years of war, no other Canadian senior officer ever trod the decks of any ships of the corvette navy that I served in, and even a commander was a rare event indeed.

Corvette crews were young; officers and men were mostly right out of high school, and anyone over thirty found himself nicknamed "Pappy" and the oldest man in the ship. Consequently, corvette people were all junior in rank and rate, most of their upper-deck crews being ordinary seamen, and with leading seamen often carrying out the jobs normally assigned petty officers, and the engine rooms filled with youngsters right out of mechanical training school. Early in the war, a corvette would be commanded by a Naval Reserve (ex-merchant navy) lieutenant, with a Volunteer Reserve lieutenant as executive officer or "Jimmy the One", and two other officers—junior lieutenants or sublieutenants—as watch-keepers. The corvettes were cobbled together, half a dozen at a time, into escort groups, led by an old destroyer usually commanded by a lieutenant or lieutenant-commander of either the RCN or, especially in the early days, the RN.

When you first joined a ship in the corvette navy, you passed from one world into another. You left behind the Big Navy, where you had done your training, the shoreside navy with all its braid and bands and bumf, and you joined an outfit that was run along the lines of a small corner-store. For corvette types were "family"; you soon got to know the characters in your own ship, and in the others of the group. There were chummy ships, whose destinies seemed always to be bound up with yours, and there were rivals, usually commanded by officers senior to your own. Months would go by, grow into years; the shoreside navy became a memory, although there were always officers and men joining ship for a trip or two before going back ashore to the other world where they were busy building careers.

For most of us, the corvettes, the frigates, the Bangors, and the old four-stackers and other obsolete destroyers of the escort fleet became home.

At the end of the war, some of the fellows I'd stood watch with in the early days were still around, most of them in different ships, in different jobs, but still accustomed to spending their days slumped against a bridge dodger, with an elbow hooked around a voice-pipe while the old bucket rolled her guts out beneath them. The corvette navy was more a way of life than anything else.

It was a way of life a world away from anything the Real Canadian Navy had envisaged, and the training accorded us reflected the gap between the two. With dozens of other keen young types, I'd done a course at the Royal Military College's Stone Frigate in Kingston, at that time the only naval officers' training establishment available in the country. We were trained there to take our places in the Grand Fleet that fought at Jutland a generation before; we became proficient, after hours on the parade ground, at drilling in fours, only to find when we emerged that some brass-hat had changed the rules and everyone had switched over to drilling in threes. We were none of us much good on parade grounds after that, and gunner's mates, those spit-and-polish tyrants, were an especial nightmare. To this day I can recall with real fright the fearful aspect of a veteran gunner's mate whose attention had been drawn to the wavering performance of a platoon led by myself during morning divisions on the parade ground at Esquimalt. Divisions is the morning ceremonial parade that begins the day in big ships or land bases of the Real Navy, full of stamping feet and shouted commands and brass bands, and, when properly done, is pretty stirring stuff, what with all those gaiters and bayonets and bugles. My lot, a raw bunch of new entries fresh from Brandon and Swift Current, lacked the snap and precision of the Brigade of Guards, and after drawing upon ourselves the censure of the gunner presiding on the dais, we were horrified to see the burly form of the most irascible of all the gunner's mates descending upon us, black as a thundercloud.

In a moment he was in our midst; I can see him now as he ducked down so that he was invisible to the official eyes on the dais. He marched along backwards, bent over like some malevolent Quasimodo, and mouthed at us in a sort of hiss that pierced us to our chicken hearts. He was a fearsome sight; his eyes glared at us from beneath beetling brows, his visage was like raw, bloody beef (he was reputed to shave with an axe), and his features were contorted with a rage he seemed able to assume instantly, at will.

"If you effing young bastards don't effing well smarten up, by the holy old Jesus I'll have your effing guts for my effing garters," he said, and made violent pulling motions with his hamlike hands.

No words could convey the infinite menace of that fearful

figure, its red face, pocked and seamed by years of exotic excess with the China squadron, thrust into the pale ranks of my pimply schoolboys. Having imparted his frightful warning, he vanished from our midst like some pantomime demon; doubling smartly to one side, he resumed his position on the perimeter of the parade ground, a rigid, upright figure staring unseeingly to his front, his thumbs behind the seams of his trousers.

God, how we marched, ashen-faced and green of gill, through the remainder of that ghastly rigadoon.

Not the least of the attractions of the escort navy was that parades of any sort played no part in its daily routine. In corvettes, we did not parade; we "fell in" and "fell out", and life was immeasurably eased thereby.

It was the same with just about everything the Big Navy imparted to us. A dear old stick of an Edwardian naval officer, gallantly returned to duty after years of retirement, initiated us into the mysteries of celestial navigation, using a sextant and a laborious system of sines and cosines which took hours to work out, and with which any of Nelson's officers would have been familiar.

We used to be tested in our proficiency by being sent out to establish the position of the RMC jetty with a series of star sights, but such was the toil involved that many of us—I blush to admit it—preferred to work it out backwards. After all, we *knew* where we were; we simply looked up our latitude and longitude and worked backwards through the tables to find what our sextant angles should have been, with a trifling error added to impart verisimilitude; too precise an observation might arouse suspicion.

Our instructor was old and tired; so tired that the circles which he endlessly chalked on the blackboard all ended as untidy ellipses, and he mumbled and muttered rather than spoke, communication being rendered even more difficult by a plummy upper-class accent. Inevitably, he was known to all as "Rumbleguts", and it was widely affirmed that he never spoke, he simply opened his mouth and let his guts rumble.

"From this point—heah—" he would mumble, his chalk screeching dustily, "we draw a line down to—" and a dozen of us, heads bent over desks, would interpolate for him with the unconscious cruelty of youth an audible "thayah". He was a delightful old party, beloved of us all, but when we went to sea we found that the escort navy navigated by the new air-force "intercept" method, an infinitely faster and simpler technique; all Rumbleguts' laborious processes became just a memory among the chalk dust.

Even our warlike exercises, enormously enjoyed at the time, proved to have little practical application in the curious force we were destined to join. Revolver practice had a particular attraction for us; in my mind's eye, I pictured myself, Webley in hand, waving my gallant lads on as we swarmed over the decks of some cringing foeman. Alas for reality; in all my years in the small-ship navy the only non-practice revolver shot I heard was that fired in the dark watches of a refit port by a bored sentry who got to fiddling with the revolver in his belt and put a bullet in his foot, thereafter being reduced to carrying an empty weapon, with the bullets in his pocket.

But gunnery school was the highlight of our training, the very heart and essence of the Big Navy. Everything was done with snap and precision; we moved at the double, and the moment we halted, anywhere, we would number off or dress our line or sort ourselves out according to height. (Tallest on the left, shortest on the right, *size*!) My particular day-dream grew out of the calm precision which prevailed in the big-ship gunnery communication we practised in school, with each gun in a ship's armament reporting its state, in set ritual phrases, to a central control transmitting station, called "T.S.", deep in the armoured bowels of a great battleship.

"Number One gun, T.S.," the rating from Number One gun would call.

"T.S. Number One gun," the transmitting station officer would reply.

"Number One gun cleared away, bore clear." And so each gun would report in, ready for action, as the turrets trained around and the mighty ship prepared to annihilate some distant foe. Then would come the thrilling command: "All guns, with a full charge and armour-piercing shell, load! Load! Load!"

In the clinical calm of the transmitting station of the gunnery school, we would be borne into battle with the chanted orders and responses intoned like some litany, and in our daydreams we saw ourselves at our moment of triumph or glorious sacrifice, serene and unruffled in the eye of the storm.

The reality of corvette gunnery was a fearful blow. The gun on our fo'c'sle, a four-inch, turn-of-the-century antique, was a sad come-down from all the gleaming monsters of gunnery school, but it remained for our first gunnery action to completely dispel my dreams of glory. There'd been a fearful bang in the convoy one dark and windy night, and as we tumbled up to our crowded bridge the captain was sucking his teeth and wondering audibly what the hell the hold-up was with the bloody star shell, for we were by now supposed to be illuminating our sector of water in search of a surfaced U-boat.

Stung into fury, our bearded Number One, who was also gunnery officer, leaned over the canvas dodger and addressed the blackness below, where rattles and bangs and muffled oaths indicated the gun's crew was clearing for action.

"Get cracking with that effing gun," he roared, "or I'll come down there and boot your effing backsides up through your effing teeth!" So much for the ordered calm, the chanted litany, the unruffled precision of the gunnery world in the escort navy.

Yet, for all that, the Big Navy taught us much that was of use: seamanship and signalling, pilotage and boatwork. ("What a shower of useless clots," our hardcase old Petty Officer instructor had moaned as he watched us, oars astraddle, attempting to come alongside. "You come crawling up like an effing great spider!") Most important of all, it taught us pride; a great, overweening pride in the Navy, the best, the oldest, the senior service, and in our association with the Royal Navy, *the* navy, with its glorious traditions of victory going back into the mists of time. It was not taught us in class, but was simply acquired by a sort of osmosis; one picked it up unconsciously from association with instructors steeped in the Old Navy, and of all the lessons learned ashore, it stood us in greatest stead at sea.

There was little enough to be proud of in the early days of the corvette navy. With experience and direction in such short supply, everything in a corvette depended upon the character and competence of the captain. If you were fortunate enough, as I was, to serve in a new ship commanded by an experienced merchant seaman, able to adapt to naval routines, you were one of a lucky minority; most of the new ships in the early months of the war were a shambles, and some were downright disgraceful. There was incompetence of every sort, at every level; some of the ships were barely able to get to sea, and once there, were fortunate to find their way back to port without mishap. Indiscipline was chronic, drunken captains, useless officers, mutinous crews were commonplace; those of us in well-run ships grew to dread the prospect of new Canadian corvettes joining our group and tarnishing our Canadian image in the eyes of thunderstruck friends in British ships or bases. It was often all too easy to pick out the Canadian from a group of corvettes alongside; she was the dirty one with rusty sides, and with half her crew in tattered clothes of every sort, playing catch on the jetty.

But with the passage of time and growing experience, we Canadians came of age. The drunks, the cowards, the incompetents wheedled berths ashore; abler officers took command and abler men qualified as leading seamen and petty officers. Discipline, and with it the contentment of crews and the efficiency of ships, improved tremendously, and once they had acquired the confidence born of experience, the superior education and intelligence of Canadian crews began to make itself felt. In the closing years of the war, Canadian frigates and corvettes were conceded to be the best there were, and the maple leaf on the funnel, the unofficial emblem first adopted by Canadian ships abroad, indicated the new pride in their nationality.

It was in these years that a new relationship developed between Canada's two navies. As the new techniques of antisubmarine warfare evolved, it was the reservists afloat in the corvettes who achieved expertise in mastering their challenge; people like Nelson Earl, Canada's top seagoing anti-sub officer. By the war's end, the best and most highly qualified specialists were reservists to a man. The endless versions of asdic (sonar) sets, the development of creeping attacks, of hedgehog and limbo ahead-throwing weapons, of high-frequency direction-finding, of VHF communication, of radar and acoustic torpedoes and sono-buoys; all these familiar features of the escort navy were a closed book to old-line officers of the Big Navy ashore, save for a handful at sea in destroyers.

But not only ships and weapons had changed since the Big Navy came ashore; crews had changed too, both in character and in competence. The new discipline of the escort groups was based on a team concept, rather than on rank structure; as in a bomber aircraft, officers and men worked in close association in positions that were often interchangeable. In such a context, the old parade-ground discipline was out of place; officers did not bellow orders to acquiescent automatons. In a sub hunt, the directing officer sought information from this rating, passed an instruction to that one, listened to a caution or suggestion from another. All were engaged in a common effort to resolve an urgent problem. It was commonplace to hear the officer directing a hunt steady his team of operators and plotters much as a coach might steady his team: "All right, fellows, let's steady down and take this baby!"

Nobody saluted anyone in a corvette at sea, yet there was unquestioned obedience throughout any well-run ship. It was a discipline based on respect, and a hierarchy based on responsibility rather than on social order.

The old discipline of the Big Navy, inherited from the Royal Navy, was based on an officer class whose education, character, and social background were worlds removed from those of the seamen. On the lower deck, thought was not encouraged; a man did as little as he could get away with, and the whole disciplinary system was geared to produce an acceptable standard of performance from an indifferent crew. It was a system measured in outward show, with lots of stamping and shouting and saluting.

But a new discipline evolved in the North Atlantic escort ships. It stemmed from the fact that, in many cases, officers and men came from the same level of society; often they lived across from one another in the same street, had attended the same schools. There was still the old need for obedience and deference to responsibility, but it could no longer be based on the class structure of the old-fashioned navy, or on the system of enforcement through marine guards and regulating officers and the noncommissioned hierarchy of big-ship routine. The new escort-ship discipline was effective, if not showy. Officers were still segregated from men, an essential to any discipline, but they ate the same food, prepared in the same galley, in the wardroom as on the messdecks.

When the Big Navy attempted to enforce the old discipline in the old way as it returned to sea in the big cruisers and carriers at last available at the war's end, it ran into trouble. A dashing pre-war destroyer officer found himself unable to command a Tribal-class destroyer when he returned to sea late in the war, and was taken ashore with his crew in a state of mutiny. Trouble persisted after the war, but this time it was the professionals who found themselves learning from the amateurs. For in the end it was the team-style discipline, developed in the escort navy, which prevailed in both Britain's Royal Navy and the Royal Canadian Navy, and this acceptance was an indication of the curious reversal of roles between amateur and professional which had taken place during the war years. For the Battle of the Atlantic turned its amateur reservists into the true professionals of antisubmarine warfare, and reduced the shore-bound officers of the Big Navy to beginners who had to re-learn their trade before they were fit to go back to sea. In the North Atlantic, the little-ship navy had become Number One.

3
SLIP AND PROCEED

〰〰〰〰〰〰〰〰〰〰〰〰〰〰〰〰〰〰〰〰〰〰

"Four-thirty, sir!"

We are snatched from the warm world of sleep by the rough hand on our shoulder and start up, blinded by the light, to find the quartermaster, cowled and hooded like a medieval monk in his fleece-lined watch-coat, bending over us. For some reason which we never understand, Operations ashore always sail escorts at some ghastly hour, never quite night or quite day; it is part of the traditional horror of sailing day. Always it is the same: the stuffy cabin, the dazzling light on the white paintwork, the oppressive, all-pervading sense of foreboding, the certain knowledge of misery to come.

Pull on the old sea-going uniform; hump yourself into the heavy winter sheepskin, stiff with salt, and the zip-fastened flying-boots, while overhead the thumps and muffled bumpings tell that the deck party is going about its work of "singling up". The heavy ropes, stiff with frost and black with use, are being lifted off the wharfside bollards in readiness for departure, leaving us secured by only a single set of warps to the shore: head and stern lines, breasts and springs. The after winch gives a few appropriately hollow groans before reluctantly settling down to its task of reeling in the frozen weight of the stern lines; you can hear the voice of the leading hand as he directs their stowage under the pom-pom bandstand. Bells clang deep in the bowels of the ship; they are testing the engine-room telegraphs and bridge communications as His Majesty's Canadian Ship *Trail* prepares for sea.

Out on deck it is black as Toby's arse, as a cowled figure remarks as we make our way forward; that is Bill Harvey, the sublieutenant in charge of the quarterdeck party. There is a light dusting of snow on the steel deck, making it dangerously slippery, and as we climb the steel ladders up to the bridge we become aware of the biting wind whistling in from the east. God, it'll be nasty outside with this gale still blowing! The sudden serenity of the asdic cabin is welcome; Clarke, the HSD and the senior asdic rating aboard, is checking out his set, and the chart table behind its black-out curtains is a warm pool of light. It's all there, just as it was laid out yesterday: the chart, with its pencilled course from St. John's to the rendezvous point where we're to meet our convoy well out in the Atlantic, south of Cape Race; the notebook, with its estimated courses and speeds and times of arrival, in accordance with the secret signal received from Operations the day before, its traditional preamble going back to the days of Pepys's navy: "Being in all respects ready for sea, slip and proceed at 0500. . . ."

"Hands to stations for leaving harbour!" That's the bosun's mate making the pipe through the crowded messdecks, and already the fo'c'sle is alive with hooded figures. There's the captain coming up onto the bridge, and we make way for him as he peers over the dodger into the icy blackness. The tug has hauled off the two sleeping corvettes that have been berthed outside us; at the corvette berths, ships are crowded three and four deep alongside and at the trot-buoys in the centre of the harbour. Figures take their accustomed places; the yeoman of signals takes charge of his signalmen, and from the bridge-wing voice-pipe a steady voice announced from the wheelhouse: "Coxswain at the wheel, sir!"

The engines are rung to standby; at a word from the captain, all the lines aft are cast loose and hauled in, the headline is taken in, and men stand by with fenders along the break of the fo'c'sle as the captain orders slow ahead. We are steaming against the spring line, which alone attaches us to the shore; the torque of the propeller turning over slowly walks the stern out from the wharf. When it is well clear, the captain stops engines, then orders slow astern, with the helm amidships. Responsive as a motorboat, the ship begins to gather sternway; the wharf slips by with gathering speed as the siren blasts three times to warn any traffic that we are proceeding in reverse. The helm is put over and the stern moves obediently to starboard until we lie in midstream, our bows pointing toward the wharf, where the tug is already returning the two outer corvettes to the berth we have just vacated. The engines are stopped, and we lie silently, still turning, our sidelights gleaming red and green in the oily water beneath. Then "Half ahead", and the ship swings rapidly as the rudder bites under the impetus of our new momentum, and we steady with our head pointing directly at the distant harbour entrance. Now the wind is strong and cold, blowing directly into our faces. Below us the fo'c'sle party is already stowing lines and fenders, securing for sea; in daylight, they would have been fallen into line, facing to port, like the seamen on the quarterdeck, ready to honour the Admiral's flag when the bosun's pipe shrilled the "Still".

Ahead of us, a confusion of dim lights shows where our sisters of the escort group are leaving their berths; we stop and wait while they sort themselves out. That will be HMS *Montgomery,* the old four-funnelled former American destroyer, built late in the First World War and handed over to the Royal Navy in the destroyers-for-bases deal. Her captain, a professional RN lieutenant-commander, is our senior officer, and he leads the parade as he takes us out to sea: five Canadian corvettes and a Juicer four-stacker, a typical mid-ocean escort group in this winter of 1941-42.

All about us is the sleeping city of St. John's; the barren hills of the South Side rise unseen to starboard; the snow-dusted streets gleaming fitfully in the lights of a passing car are all we can make out of the city itself, climbing its hills all along our port side. There is enough light to pick out the rocks of the narrow entrance: the dim, flashing light of Chain Rock to port and the concrete bulges of the entrance battery burrowed into the rock to starboard. As we reach the entrance, a red signal-light blinks blearily from the ship ahead: "Order One, speed 12 knots." We find our place in the line-ahead formation, crank up the engine revolutions for 12 knots, and we are off and running.

In Newfyjohn, as the sailors call St. John's, you are either in the harbour or out of it; there is no long estuary leading to the sea. The transition is brief and dramatic; one moment you are trundling along in the comparative serenity of harbour, and the next you are in the open ocean, amid all the fury of the North Atlantic winter. As we leave the narrow entrance, we stick our bows into a great black sea, and we climb upwards, only to come crashing dizzily down in a welter of breaking water. We ship the end of a sea over the bows just as the fo'c'sle party is putting the finishing touches on the securing of the upper-deck gear, and they scuttle for safety in their sodden sheepskins, in a flurry of boots and bad language. The sea is getting up under the impetus of that shrieking wind; for the next few hours we shall be punching into the teeth of the freshening gale, and already a lot of us are having sudden doubts about our stomachs. There are retching sounds from behind us on the bridge, where one of the new signalmen is bringing up his innards as he greets his first Atlantic gale; in anticipation, the yeoman has thoughtfully provided a bucket lashed to a stanchion, and I can feel my own stomach heave in sympathy.

I mentally review what I had for dinner last night. We'd had a couple of rums in the Crowsnest, that marvellously contrived club for seagoing officers on the draughty upper floor of a Water St. warehouse, before going on to the New-foundland Hotel for the traditional last-night bang-up dinner. We'd dined in sombre state in the great, glacial dining-room, topping off a fine dinner with Drambuie, sipping that amber ambrosia in order, we assured ourselves, to settle the stomach. Two of our five at dinner had Scots blood in them, and they assured us that Scots never drank for pleasure; it would be contrary to their dour Presbyterian upbringing. But it was only prudent, mind, to take a wee drop to whet the appetite or settle the stomach, to aid digestion or steady the hand, so to speak. We had, accordingly, taken prudent precautions, but as the ship crashed and plunged into the rising head sea and the signalman behind retched and gasped, I wondered if we had been prudent enough.

Once clear of the harbour, the watch closed up to begin the seagoing routine which would last until we berthed on the other side of the Atlantic; one-third of the ship's company manning the engines, boilers, wheel, asdic, wireless, and look-out positions, the other two-thirds below trying to catch what sleep they could before their own four-hour stint began. It is my watch until eight, but the captain lingers anxiously, wor-ried about the rising wind and sea.

A green one crashes aboard; peering over the dodger we can see its dark shape engulf our foredeck, and we crouch for shelter as the ship plunges thunderously into it. A wall of water, tons of it, sweeps across our fo'c'sle to hurl itself against our bridge structure with a resounding thump. Water sweeps overhead; even in the shelter of the dodger we are drenched, and from below comes a series of bangs and crashes, from messdecks and galley and upper deck, where a hundred items, big and small, have bumped and smashed and clanged and rattled under the impact of the heavy sea. A great murmur of protest, of oaths and groans and bitching, rises from the ventilators and voice-pipes, and from the wheelhouse we hear the bosun's mate, loud and clear: "This effing bucket! Roll on, our refit!"

The captain grins, catches my eye: "Hearts of oak!" he grunts.

But it is clear that we cannot go on bashing into it at this speed. Up ahead *Montgomery* must be semi-submerged, those old fourpipers being notoriously the world's worst sea-boats. Sure enough, back comes the signal: reduce speed to 10 knots. It is going to be a long run, just to meet our convoy, and it has all the earmarks of another sticky crossing.

For us, our watch eventually comes to an end, as they always do; we hand over to Bill Harvey, his face still puffy from sleep, and give him our course and speed and show him our position on the chart. A last look round before going below. A grey, lumpy sea, flecked with white, fills our universe, under grey, scudding clouds. There is no land to be seen, anywhere, only our little handful of ships in all this mad world of wind and sea and driven water. We are steaming in line abreast now, at intervals of a mile. There is *Arvida* to starboard, and to port are *Chilliwack* and *Dauphin* and *Kamsack*, with *Montgomery* just visible, now and again, far on the horizon beyond. But although the sea is worse than ever, the wind seems to be dropping, not quite so fierce as it seemed at the beginning of our watch. But then, the wind never *does* seem so bad at the end of your watch as it does at the beginning.

Breakfast in the wardroom below is a cheerless affair; the deadlights dogged down over the ports and the carpet stowed away, as it will be until we make port again, reduce the cheerful clubroom of our dockside days to a sort of clinical tank. The big armchairs are lashed to stanchions to keep them from crashing about, and we eat our greasy egg and tomato, our burnt toast and marmalade sitting bolt upright on the hard leather settee which runs along one side of the table. Number One is just finishing his breakfast as we arrive for ours, and is off to go rounds of the messdecks with the coxswain.

Better him than me! The messdecks of a corvette in bad weather are indescribable; it would be difficult to imagine such concentrated misery anywhere else. Into two triangular compartments, about 33 feet by 22 feet at their greatest di-

mensions, are crammed some sixty-odd men; each has for his
living space—eating, sleeping, relaxing—a seat on the cush-
ioned bench which runs around the outside perimeter of each
messdeck. There is a locker beneath the seat for his clothing,
and a metal ditty-box—something like an old-fashioned hat-
box—holds his personal things in a rack above. The space
where he slings his hammock—carefully selected by the older
hands and jealously guarded—is 18 inches beneath the deckhead, or another hammock, which are slung in tiers between
stanchions and beneath pipes, wherever there is room. Most
of the deck space is taken up with scrubbed deal tables, one
to each mess, where you eat or write or play interminable
games of cards.

Crowded in harbour and stuffy, the messdecks at sea are
like some vision of Hades. There is absolutely no fresh air;
all the ports, open in harbour, are dogged down and blanked
over at sea, and in heavy weather even the cowl ventilators
from the upper deck have to be sealed off. Dim emergency
lights, red or blue, provide the only illumination in the dark
hours, and around the clock there is always at least one
watch trying to catch a few hours of oblivion, while about
them the life of the mess goes on: men coming and going
from outside, or snatching a meal before going on watch.
With the hammocks slung, there is hardly room anywhere to
stand upright, and there is moisture everywhere—water swirling in over the coamings when the outside doors open,
sweating from the chilled steel of the ship's side, oozing from
the countless pipe joints and deck-welds and rivets and deck
openings, and all the other manifold places where water
forces an entrance from the gale outside. Plunging into a
head sea, the noise and motion in the fo'c'sle must be experienced to be believed; a constant roar of turbulence, wind, and
water, punctuated by a crashing thud as the bow bites into
another great sea, while the whole little world is uplifted—
up, up, up—only to come crashing down as the ship plunges
her bows over and downward, to land with an impact which
hurls anyone and anything not firmly secured down to the
forward bulkhead. With a rolling, corkscrew motion, the
nightmare world of the fo'c'sle starts to climb again, up, up,
up. . . . In their navel pipes, the twin anchor cables rattle
and clank at each movement, a dominant note in the endless,
maddening din.

In such a place, under such conditions, corvette crews endure for days, weeks, years, a degree of discomfort and hard-

ship which they could not have sustained for an hour in civilian life; wet, cold, bruised, sleeping in their clothes, with never a moment's privacy or quiet. When they are keeping watch, getting up at all hours to brave the elements, night blurs into day in a misery too great for words. In everyone's mind is the surcease to come when we make port, when the motion and misery stop, and everyone can sleep, sleep, without interruption. No one thinks beyond that; to endure this crossing is our chief aim, and the ship is impelled onward by the mind and heart of every soul aboard.

But there are degrees of misery, as with anything else; when eventually the long bash to windward is done and we reach the point of rendezvous, we turn to comb the track along which the convoy will come. We are taking the seas on the quarter now, and while the ship rolls heavily, right over on her ear, there is no more pitching, and the surcease is like a kind of heaven. The wind is easing and everyone is more cheerful. Life settles into its accustomed seagoing routine; the seasick are either better now or beyond hope. In every escort, there are always one or two individuals, the chronically seasick, whose endurance becomes a matter of proud boasting by their shipmates, and who live at sea in a sort of half-world, between life and death, sustained only by a handful of crackers or soup for all the days and weeks of a voyage. Seasickness—real seasickness—is endured by these few with a resolute bravery that sometimes awes their heedless and healthy shipmates.

We have arrived at our rendezvous on time, but the convoy is a little late, delayed by weather. We are now at Westomp—Western Ocean Meeting Point—where the convoys change escorts, much as trains change crews ashore at divisional points. Our eastbound convoy here will shed the Local Escort Group which has brought it from New York, Boston, and Halifax to this point, to be replaced by us, the Mid-Ocean Escort, who will stay with it until relieved by the United Kingdom escort somewhere south of Iceland and west of Ireland.

And suddenly, there they are. First the cluttered mast of a destroyer pierces the horizon right ahead, then her whole bridge heaves into view; her signal lamp flashes a greeting, to which *Montgomery* responds. Now, right across the horizon, masts and funnels appear, rapidly climbing over the heaving seascape to reveal themselves as merchant ships; out on each flank is the tiny silhouette of an escort.

A convoy at sea is an awe-inspiring sight, even to us, who spend most of our days at sea hanging about the flanks of them, and as we draw rapidly up to this one, even off-duty crewmen climb out on our deck to have a close-hand look at HX 142, as it has been officially designated—forty-two ships, bound from Halifax to the United Kingdom with food, weapons, machinery, oil, petroleum, and all the manifold munitions of war.

A convoy is a live thing, a collective entity greater than the sum of its parts. There is an unmistakable sense of purpose about this enormous collection of ships as it forges relentlessly to the eastward, its vast bulk covering the sea from horizon to horizon. Its ships are in nine ordered ranks, its flanks five ships deep, and as we draw closer to its starboard wing we can make out the individual ships, the characters of the convoy, so to speak, whose eccentricities of appearance and behaviour are to become a part of our lives in the long days and nights ahead.

It is always a thrill to see a convoy at sea in the brief role of spectator before one's horizon becomes limited by responsibility for some single sector, and as we pass down the side of the great armada we are again moved by its sense of might and purpose, and by an appreciation of the enormous human energy and miracles of organization which have assembled this force of great ships, flying the flags of virtually every maritime nation, bound from ports all over the world to an embattled island, now besieged and surrounded. Here is one of the concentrations of power that are shaping our destiny; here in these ships are the essentials which can sustain a whole nation: food for millions of people, and fuel and arms for their defence. Millions upon millions of dollars are represented by these ships and their cargoes, the accumulated man-hours of countless men and women toiling in farms and factories in a score of countries, in hundreds of towns and cities.

This convoy, manned and escorted by more than a thousand seamen, assembled and equipped and directed by staffs who even now are plotting its position in operations rooms on both sides of the Atlantic, represents a significant portion of the wealth of the free world, the end result of millions of dedicated man-hours and a triumph of human organizing genius. More to the point, it represents a very important factor in the war between freedom and tyranny, and as we watch it surge past us we are reminded yet again of our own responsibility for its safe arrival.

The sense of power invests this collection of rusting ships with an almost elemental quality; one can sense that it will steam on, regardless of loss, regardless of weather or attack, like some great leviathan scorning the assaults of lesser creatures of the deep.

At the head of the centre column is the commodore's ship, a fine "Blue Funnel" cargo liner, one of Alfred Holt's great ships, her halyards a mass of bunting as she signals a pending course change to her charges. Behind her, sheltered by the columns on either side, are the three precious tankers carrying the fuel oil and petroleum that is perhaps the most valuable of all the varied cargoes being carried here to a besieged Britain. They are so deeply laden that they seem at times to be largely submerged, like some half-tide rocks, but as they forge into the great rollers they occasionally rise ponderously, like monstrous sea-beasts from the depths, streaming tons of water from their rusting decks.

Some of the leading ships in the columns have Spitfire and Hurricane fighters mounted on long catapult structures on their bows; these are to give us some measure of air protection as we cross "The Pit"; that enormous sector of mid-Atlantic which lies beyond the zones of air-cover extending east from Newfoundland, south from Iceland, and west from the British Isles. Strictly a one-way trip for their pilots, of course; once their job is done, the enemy aircraft shot down or driven off, they must either crash-land in the sea close to an escort and hope to be rescued from their sinking plane, or simply abandon their aircraft at a safe altitude and bail out by parachute, hoping to be plucked from the sea by an escort. Normally, escort commanders try to conserve them until sea conditions give the pilot a fighting chance of ditching or bailing out safely.

The escort carriers, converted merchantmen able to fly on and off a handful of aircraft and thus provide air cover to the convoy all the way across, are still a year in the future in this winter of '41-'42.

The ships themselves represent the whole spectrum of maritime trade. Although we do not have the older, smaller ships that sail in the slow "sc" convoys, there are ships here of every class and vintage, from trim Blue Star and Ellerman liners, still with their peacetime promenade decks amidships, to the ugly ore-carriers and the new utilitarian "Empire" and

"Fort" wartime-built ships. Mostly they are painted grey and streaked by rust and salt, but here and there are trim Scandinavians, bright in peacetime livery, with huge flags painted on their sides. Some of these neutrals still sail independently, trusting to their lights and flags to earn them safety from U-boat attack, but so many have been lost that now they tend to sail in convoy through the dangerous North Atlantic along with Allied ships.

Here and there, one can see an exotic newcomer to the grey Atlantic: a Ben liner from the Far East, a Fyffe banana boat, a Royal Mail ship from the blue Pacific, the little English Channel packet steamer sailing as rescue ship to the convoy.

We notice something missing: there's no battleship escort to give big-gun protection against a surface raider. We've grown accustomed to having one of the old "R"-class battleships, usually HMS *Revenge*, along for the ride across, but this time we've got an armed merchant cruiser, a former liner armed with six-inch guns, to add a bit of punch to the escort. Somebody makes out her name; it's *Worcestershire*, the fine old Biddy liner, and the name brings a grin all around on the bridge. For *Worcestershire* is famous for an incident involving her doctor's hideous revenge on a group of Canadian army officers who had taken passage aboard.

The doctor, who, as is traditional in HM ships, was secretary of the wardroom mess, had cautioned the Canadian army types against what he considered excessive drinking, and muttered darkly about damage to the kidneys and other possible effects. The Canadians, enjoying a respite from their usual responsibilities, were in no mood to heed these mutterings from the doctor, and when they discovered that he was a teetotaller and at the same time in charge of wardroom wines and spirits, their merriment knew no bounds. Goaded by their incessant teasing, the doctor determined to wreck a horrible revenge. With the considerable resources of the ship's big peacetime passenger dispensary at hand, he began to introduce into the Canadians' drink and food a chemical compound which turned their urine a bright orange.

This had no noticeable effect on the Canadians, other than a marked aversion to oranges and citrus fruits, so the doctor played his second card. He switched to a compound which changed his victims' water to a vivid green, and after a few days, to a rather attractive electric blue. He was now producing real results; green slowed the Canadian drinking to a trickle, and blue brought it to an absolute standstill; the Canadians sat about the wardroom morose and silent, each man alone with his thoughts, and waving away any proffered drinks which the doctor, now assiduous, pressed upon them. Pale and wan and worried, they were a pitiful sight.

But by now the doctor's blood was up; not content with the sad state to which he had reduced his hapless victims, he determined on one final brutal stroke to complete his revenge. Overnight he changed their urine to a deep black.

It was the last straw. With half-remembered tales of black-water fever crowding to their fevered minds, and pale from lack of sleep, the Canadian officers one by one called in at the ship's hospital in the morning "to have a word with the doctor".

The doctor claimed that he then made it clear to his victims that it had all been a harmless prank, but the Canadians had versions of how they had extorted details of the plot from him under duress, and with promises to have him disgraced by his fellow practitioners for violation of his Hippocratic oath. However that may be, the doctor's ingenious plot has established him as a character, and has made his ship a famous and welcome addition to any North Atlantic escort force. We are pleased to have *Worcestershire* sailing with us.

Our escort group breaks up on a signal from *Montgomery*, and each of us heads for an allotted place in the screen. We work our way gingerly across the front of the oncoming herd to take our station out on the starboard flank. *Montgomery* has positioned herself, *Arvida*, and *Chilliwack* across the front of the convoy, with *Dauphin* opposite us on the port side and *Kamsack* as Tail-End Charlie covering the rear. We are stationed so as to be able, in theory at least, to cover our sector with our asdic beams overlapping, zigzagging but maintaining station on the eight-knot convoy.

We are rapidly closing *Fort William*, a steam Bangor designed as a fast fleet minesweeper but converted into an ocean escort; she is making heavy weather of the big sea still running, shipping a good deal of water over her short fo'c'sle and low quarterdeck. Her skipper is an old friend of our own captain, and as we take over from her and begin our outward leg, our captain signals: "THERE IS A VERY YOUNG, VERY PREGNANT GIRL ON THE JETTY ASKING AFTER YOU."

Back comes the prompt response: "SHE'LL JUST HAVE TO WAIT HER TURN LIKE ALL THE OTHERS."

It raises a smile as the Local Escort hauls away for the

fleshpots of St. John's, and we settle into the familiar routine
of convoy escort. Quickly our little world takes on its distinctive shape: the diminutive silhouette of *Chiliwack* far ahead,
and the five ships of the wing column stretching down our
port side. We come to know each detail of those five ships:
their silhouettes, their peculiar groupings of funnels, masts,
and derrick booms, their varying colours, and even their distinctive rust streaks and patches. There is one in particular,
the third in line, which is of special significance; a modern
motorship, she is fitted with goalpost masts to handle her
cargo, and it is the distinctive silhouette of these great rectan-
gular projections and the thick, squat funnel which makes our
job of night station-keeping easier. *Montgomery* has the only
radar yet fitted in the group; the rest of us keep station visu-
ally, zigging outward until the convoy becomes invisible behind us, then altering course in until, at the limits of our
inward leg, the convoy becomes visible to us again. On a
black, rainy night or in a shrieking blizzard, a glimpse of
those ungodly goalpost masts helps to put things in proper
perspective, and a quick bearing tells us whether we're in
proper station.

Another help to station-keeping, but a nuisance in every
other way, is the inevitable Smoky Joe, the last ship in our
line. An old coal-burner, and only just able to keep up with
her newer, faster sisters, she frequently commits the cardinal
convoy sins of straggling and making smoke, often at the
same time. She is a case-hardened tramp of First World War
vintage, her overworked stokers attempting to keep her anti-
quated engines running at close to her maximum speed on in-
ferior coal, and she quickly establishes herself as our
particular problem child. Once she falls behind, it is all she
can do to catch up, emitting clouds of black smoke which
can be spotted by a questing U-boat far over the horizon,
thus risking the survival of every ship in convoy. Yet if she
falls back beyond the escort coverage, she is herself a sitting
duck to be snapped up by the first U-boat which sights her.

Time after time, in those first days, we close her with our
loud hailer going and signal flags flying from our yard-
arm—cautioning, cajoling, pleading, threatening. To all our
exhortations, we receive the same response: a wave of acknowledgement from her skipper at the open door of her
wheelhouse. We want him to do the best he can, but of
course we know what he is trying to cope with, and for all
our lecturing we feel a deep sympathy for his predicament.

But he is Trouble, the weak link which could mean disaster for us all, and we curse the officer ashore who included him in our lot instead of grouping him with the slower ships where he belongs.

Slowly, painfully, HX 142 inches eastward; the noon positions crawl across the chart of the western ocean in half a hundred chart rooms. Each day at noon Howard Wallace, our diminutive red-bearded navigator, emerges, sextant in hand, in the hope that the constant cloud cover will thin enough for him to get a noon altitude and thus establish our latitude, to complement the occasional star shot he may sneak in a clear patch in the night watches. On a rolling, pitching corvette bridge, with a horizon lumpy with heavy seas, it takes both luck and skill to produce satisfactory results, and for days on end bad weather reduces us to estimating our position simply on course steered and distance run. Each midday the convoy commodore, operating from the stablest platform and with the best facilities, indicates by a flag-hoist his observed or estimated position, which automatically becomes the official one of the convoy, but every self-respecting escort and merchantman commander likes to arrive at his own independent calculation, which allows him then to sneer at the figures arrived at by the commodore.

In good weather the commodore may exercise his ships in convoy evolutions, carrying out turns by signal, or exercising gun crews in firing close-range weapons.

A convoy is like a small city at sea, full of minor or major crises: a man is injured or falls sick, and the destroyer's doctor may have to be transferred to a merchantman—not fun in bad weather; one ship has engine trouble, another has a bad leak, or problems with cargo shifting. There is a constant flow of information back and forth between commodore and convoy, convoy and escort. Daily our senior officer checks out the fuel remaining to each escort; under the best of conditions some of them, particularly destroyers, can only just make the other side of a mid-ocean crossing with a slim margin of fuel remaining, so that bad weather or prolonged high-speed steaming means refuelling at sea, always a bit dicey in bad weather. But the overriding concerns, overshadowing all else, are weather and U-boats, and threatening situations in connection with either call for consultation between commodore and escort.

Each evening our wireless office gives us the latest Admiralty appreciation of the U-boat situation. Daily, with Teutonic punctuality, each U-boat at sea tries to signal Doenitz's headquarters its position and situation, so that the master in his Berlin bunker may guide them to a chosen target. These U-boat transmissions are monitored by shore stations in Britain, their messages decoded by the secret "Ultra" deciphering machine, and the position of each U-boat is plotted and broadcast to Allied escorts. Each evening, as we crawl steadily eastward, we plot the positions of known U-boats on our chart, and it becomes ever more apparent that we are in for a brush with them; half a dozen are scattered right across our path, and although we are routed ever more to the north, up toward the Arctic Circle itself, no amount of course alteration seems able to take us clear. Bad weather, which makes it impossible for U-boats to operate on the surface, may yet see us through. And bad weather there is in plenty.

Gale after gale shrieks down upon us, howling out of the north as we approach Cape Farewell, southernmost tip of Greenland. Fierce winds tear at our rigging, snatch the tops off waves and send them flying above our mastheads, stinging our faces and blinding our eyes. Mountainous seas crash inboard, making our upper decks impassable, sweeping over our forward gun and crashing against our superstructure with an impact that jars us to the keel. Life below is a hell of wet clothes and fitful sleep, of sandwich meals and constant violent, bruising motion. Even the plumbing is impossible; to use the toilet is to risk a cold douche as the head seas overpower valves and piping.

On a wild night watch, I see the lighter rim of the sky blotted out and realize, in a moment of mind-numbing panic, that the wall of blackness that towers ahead of us is an enormous, an unbelievable, sea, the "67th wave" dreaded by every sailor. I duck beneath the dodger as the bows rise, and commend my soul to God. There is a thunderous roar, and the whole world is blotted out in water, filled with a myriad crashes and crackings. Miraculously, the wave passes, and I emerge, soaked and scared yet unscathed. But in the sudden silence I can sense something wrong: the ship is falling off into the trough and I can get no answer from the wheelhouse voice-pipe. Mad with fright—if the ship falls broadside to the waves in this mountainous sea we shall surely be rolled right over—I dash down the ladder and burst into the wheelhouse, and into a scene of utter chaos. The rogue sea had burst in the shutters and windows of the wheelhouse, flooding and gutting it and knocking helmsman and telegraph rating against the after bulkhead. They are still there, paralysed with fright and shock, but at the wheel is the captain, brought from his tiny sea-cabin off the wheelhouse, now spinning the wheel hard over to get the ship back head to sea. I ring the engines to emergency full ahead, and we wait, frozen in an agonized tableau, our eyes riveted on the pool of light that is the steering compass. The ship rolls heavily, deeply, right over on her side; if she gets another sea in this position we are all gone for sure. But the engine beat quickens; we can hear the stokehold bell below as the engine room opens all the taps, and at last we can see the compass card begin to move. The crisis is past; it is just a matter of shoring up our shattered wheelhouse covers and we are back in business.

The wild weather may be keeping the U-boats down, but it is also taking its toll of the convoy; under its thunderous blows, HX 142 begins to disintegrate. The gaps between ships increase as ships seek greater sea-room. There is a tremendous collision near the centre as a great bulk carrier becomes unmanageable and sheers out of line, her bows colliding with those of a new Empire vessel in the adjoining column; in the black night we hear the rending screech of fractured metal above the howling of the gale.

Fortunately, it is a glancing blow, but even so it has torn a gaping hole in the starboard bow of the Empire ship, and although the hole is well above the water-line, in this wild weather it is a dangerous wound. Both ships fall astern to examine and repair damage as best they can, and *Kamsack* is told off to stand by them until they can rejoin the convoy. But there is no respite; all the next day the gaps between ships steadily widen, although the commodore has reduced speed to a signalled four knots, which is more like two over the ground. At this speed some ships are virtually unable to maintain a proper course; they fall out of line and peel off to either side, seeking sea-room. They give us in the escorts some grey hairs, for there is nothing which can bring one's heart into one's mouth faster than the sight of a great black shape looming out of the night when one fancied oneself safely distant a mile or so from the nearest merchantman. Next morning Smoky Joe is far behind, now just a smudge of smoke astern on the horizon, and *Kamsack* is directed by *Montgomery* to take him under her wing as well. By the morning of this third day of the gale, HX 142 is scattered over miles of ocean, its shattered ranks broken into two shapeless huddles of storm-lashed ships, its escorts now running dangerously low on fuel with a thousand miles of stormy Atlantic still ahead and the U-boat gauntlet still to run.

Fortunately, at this desperate juncture the wind begins to ease; by afternoon it is no more than a fresh breeze and by nightfall the enormous sea has begun to subside. Dawn next day reveals a North Atlantic restored to something like normalcy. Immediately *Montgomery* drops back to fuel from the aftermost tanker in the centre column, signalling as she goes the rotation in which we, the other escorts, are to leave the screen to top up our depleted tanks. By mid-afternoon our turn has come; we steam down through the re-forming ranks of the convoy and approach the tanker from astern. Our fo'c'sle party grapples and picks up the long grass-line streamed behind the huge tanker, together with the empty water-breaker used as a buoy on the end of it, and haul it on the empty fuel hose, filled with air so it will float, which the tanker pays out like a great serpent astern. We close up until we are broad on the tanker's quarter, the buoyant hose streaming astern of the tanker and then up onto our fo'c'sle in a deep U-shape. The hose end is quickly fastened to the pipe-nozzle which had just been fitted for the purpose at our refit last fall, and at a flat signal from us the oiler begins pumping. We steam along at convoy speed, protected from attack by ships all about us, keeping station easily by maintaining the U in the bight of the hose, which in effect cushions any small failure in station-keeping caused by wind or sea.

This is a method of fuelling at sea developed by mid-ocean escorts in the teeth of regular-navy opposition, for in peacetime oiling had been regarded as an evolution, something to be carried out on calm seas as a display of smart seamanship. Destroyers were required to close the tanker alongside and to steam, beam to beam, a few feet apart, while a short length of hose was passed directly across. Station-keeping had to be perfect; the slightest yawing resulted in a broken hose or a collision, sometimes both together, so that the evolution became impossible with any sort of sea running. Even the astern method had its dangers; more than one escort had been covered with thick black oil from bows to bridge, from masthead to water-line, as a result of a hose breaking during fuelling and the broken end, flying madly about under great pressure, squirting tons of heavy bunker oil over everything.

Such a nightmare was always possible in bad weather, but the large amount of slack in the fuel hose represented by the deep U-shaped bight provided a safe degree of leeway for any well-handled ship. In less than an hour we have topped-up, had pumping stopped, let the hose blow clear, capped it, and cast it off, and we are on our way back to our screening position on the starboard flank of the convoy.

All day HX 142 has been re-forming, the commodore maintaining slow speed while stragglers hurry back into position, and the ranks slowly close up and regain cohesion. Last to return is Smoky Joe, clouds of smoke belching from his tall, thin funnel. As night closes in, convoy speed is increased.

Next day brings a new enemy. We are approaching the area, just beyond reach of air cover from Iceland or Ireland, where the U-boats maintain their patrolling line. It is a thin affair nowadays, as more and more U-boats are hurried down to the happy hunting grounds off the American coast where American shipping, unprotected by convoy as a result of an almost unbelievable miscalculation by Admiral King and his staff, can be butchered like so many sheep. But the evening U-boat report shows plenty of activity still in our area, and the Admiralty, in a special signal to us, warn that at least three U-boats are in the immediate vicinity of our convoy.

We take every precaution; lookouts are especially vigilant, guns and depth-charges are checked out, and we close in to abjure Smoky Joe to throw on his best lumps of coal in order to keep in station and make the minimum amount of smoke. We receive the mandatory wave of the hand—reassuring? resigned? resentful? Who could say?—and return to our position on the screen, maintaining our zigzag in meticulous station. The night passes without incident.

Next day it becomes clear that we have been spotted. Unusual U-boat wireless activity from our immediate area indicates we are being tailed by at least one U-boat, and the pack is gathering. Late that afternoon, as visibility fades, *Montgomery* leaves her station and sweeps astern at high speed; half an hour later the commodore alters convoy course drastically to the northward. *Montgomery* hopes to force any shadower to submerge and thereby not be in a position to detect our new change of course. *Montgomery* returns early in the evening without having spotted anything, but it is hoped that we have shaken off, at least temporarily, any U-boat attack. It is standard practice for U-boats to maintain contact at visibility limit astern, on the surface or at periscope depth according to circumstances, steering convoy course and speed by day and surfacing at nightfall to overtake at high speed and gain an attacking position on the bow of the convoy. Attack is usually from this position on the surface, the boat trimmed down so that virtually only her conning tower is exposed. A spread of torpedoes is fired, with the attacker then either running right through the convoy, or turning to escape at high speed on the surface while the convoy steams on.

It is a black night; there will be a moon later on, if the cloud cover permits, but meantime the darkness favours us in our attempt to avoid detection. We steam on, everyone on tenterhooks; on the bridge and in the messdecks the tension is almost palpable. Yet at sea we are all fatalists; when I turn in after an austere supper—all our fresh supplies are long gone and we virtually live on Spam—I quickly fall into deep and dreamless sleep.

Good God, what was that? I sit upright in the pitch-black cabin. There it is again: the rumbling bang against the ship's side of an underwater explosion, and as I switch on the lamp there is another one. Not depth-charges, these; they can only be torpedoes, and as I fling my legs over the side of the bunk and pull on my seaboots, the alarm bells suddenly go off overhead, sounding action stations, and the whole sleeping ship explodes into pandemonium. Racing for the bridge, I cannon into dark figures, bulky with lifejackets; the night is filled with drumming feet, muttered curses, the metallic sounds of clips being loosened, hatches flung open, guns and depth-charges cleared away, and over all the insistent, mind-maddening clangour of the alarm bells.

Up on the bridge the atmosphere is tense with suppressed excitement; the captain is at the voice-pipes, bringing the ship around to point directly away from the convoy, his voice clipped, controlled, urgent. And the convoy, ah God, the convoy—

We must have been at the inner limit of our zigzag when the torpedoes struck; the dark shapes of the outer column tower darkly above us, seeming frighteningly close. But just beyond them is a terrifying sight: the leading ship of the second column is afire, and flames can be seen all along her upper deck. Even as we watch, there is a blinding flash, and suddenly she bursts into a towering pillar of flame. Across the water comes the sound of the explosion, and a new, horrifying sound: the roar of the inferno that has engulfed her. She must have been carrying high-octane petroleum as deck cargo; only this could have turned her into such a tremendous torch. It is as bright as day; the flames light up the sea all around us, throwing the ships of the intervening column into bold relief, illuminating the pale, tense faces on the bridge behind me. All eyes are on the doomed ship; nobody speaks, we are struck dumb by the fearful majesty of the terrible scene before us, by the unbelievable roar of the holocaust. Slowly, serenely, she passes down the column, isolated now from her grubby sisters ploughing past in the splendid beauty of her destruction. It is a voice up the pipe from the wireless office which breaks the spell: "From *Montgomery*, sir: Raspberry!"

It is an order to all escorts to turn outward and illuminate their sectors with star shell—one of the new group tactical evolutions embodied in the escort "Bible", the big blue-bound volume known as Western Approaches Convoy Instructions, or simply "Wackey". From our inward position, the captain swings our bows around until we are steaming directly away from the convoy, and at a word from him Falconer, our gunnery officer, calls down the foregun voice-pipe: "With star shell and reduced charge, load! Load! Load!" There are orderly scufflings from the gun's crew, and we can hear the breech being swung open and closed, and then Falconer passes down the arc to be covered. "Illuminate from red 45 to green 45." The gun is trained and reported ready, and as all glasses on the bridge are readied and we cover our eyes with our hands, there comes the order "Shoot!" A blinding flash, a hot whiff of cordite, and in the sudden blackness that follows, everyone peers intently out into the dark void on the port bow. After what seems ages, the shell bursts, high and far, and instantly turns night into day. As the magnesium flare, dangling from its parachute, slowly descends, it lights up the empty sea beneath it. Even as we watch, the gun fires again, and after another ageless interval, a second flare appears, further ahead, and now higher than the original, which has been drifting evenly down. And then another, and another; in the space of a minute we have hung a curtain of star shell over a wide arc of the sea, and as the flares drift lower they light up the surface in unbelievable detail, throwing into relief every tiny wavetop. All around the convoy the other escorts are lighting up their sectors; already we can benefit from the outermost star shell fired by *Chilliwack* ahead and *Kamsack* far astern. If, as *Montgomery* believes, the U-boat attacking us is making her escape on the surface, we should be able to catch a glimpse of her, with any luck. Luck, because the area to be covered is huge, and the arcs can never be simultaneous; the first star shell is dipping into the sea, to be snuffed out before the arc can be half completed, and the gaps between areas covered by individual escorts are many and large. And yet—there is a lot of light up there, a lot of sea laid bare for the scrutiny of hundreds of searching eyes. *Montgomery* has radar, a sort of Stone Age contraption; one of her officers told me that they don't put any faith in any object it reports unless they can actually see it, and that its main use was in giving a distance off the convoy for station-keeping, but for all of that they'll be chasing every back-echo and will-o'-the-wisp wavetop in reports right now.

And then—there it is! Far out to the right of the last star shell I catch a glimpse through the binoculars of something in the wavetops, and as my heart almost stops with excitement I see, for the first time, the unmistakable outline of a U-boat conning tower. My shout is simultaneous with that of the captain: "There she is: green 45!" and then everything happens at once. The captain cannons into me, leaping for the voice-pipe. "Starboard twenty!" Falconer calls for another star shell on the same bearing as the last, and Harvey rushes for the asdic set to give his operators the bearing of the surfaced enemy; the moment he dives he becomes their responsibility. As the ship steadies on her new course, heading directly for the submarine, the captain issues a string of orders. A sighting signal is cracked off to *Montgomery,* the gun's crew bangs off its last star shell and then loads with high-explosive shell and a full charge, and down in the waist and quarterdeck the depth-charge crews rush to put shallow settings on their first pattern of charges, for we hope to be up with the U-boat before he can dive deep. The captain calls for emergency full ahead, and even on the bridge we can hear the double ring of the engine telegraphs in the wheelhouse, and up the stokehold ventilators behind us we can hear the answering bells ringing and the stokers shouting as they open all the taps.

I keep the glasses glued on the U-boat, now brightly illuminated as the star-shell flares fall closer; under our feet the ship vibrates madly as the engines reach for their full power. We are closing rapidly, but suddenly there is a welter of white water all about the tiny black conning tower towards which we are charging.

She's diving! I turn to the captain, but he has already seen for himself.

"She's blowing ballast tanks," he mutters, and calmly takes a bearing of her over the standard compass.

In a matter of seconds, she is gone, her position marked by a swirl of foam, and moments later our last star shell dips into the sea and blackness locks us in on every side. The captain moves into the asdic house to direct the search, and as we approach the diving position we reduce speed to ten knots, our asdic beam searching beneath the surface for the vanished enemy.

"From *Montgomery*, sir; *Kamsack* to close and assist *Trail* in hunting U-boat," reports the signal yeoman from the wireless cabin voice-pipe. This is welcome news; with two escorts, one to hold contact while the other attacks, we should be able to kill this U-boat. On the silent bridge, on the darkened decks, men stand in attitudes of tension, all minds on the softly lit compass in the asdic cabin, where a ray of light and the persistent ping! of the set indicate that our supersonic beam is probing the blind depths for the hidden killer of our ships.

"Echo bearing red 10, range eleven hundred yards!" Out on the windswept bridge, I hear the report we have been aching to hear on the chart-room voice-pipe. The report is from the operator on the set; from Clarke, his leading hand and the ranking asdic rating on the ship, comes the qualifying report: "Echo low," and then, after the cut-offs have been established, the confident, unequivocal report: "Target is submarine, sir, on an opening course."

From the captain, then, the low words that put it all together: "Start the attack!"

The attacking signal is made to *Kamsack* and *Montgomery*, we accelerate to a fifteen-knot attacking speed, settings for depth-charges are confirmed and their crews put on standby for firing. As officer of the watch I keep a lookout on the bridge, but my mind is with the little group huddled about the soft-lit instruments inside the cabin behind me, where the operator is holding contact, Clarke, our senior specialist, is keeping the captain posted, and the deep black marks of the chemical traces mark the roll of paper on the set each time an echo is received back from the U-boat, and thus indicate its range on the marked scale.

Bang!

Jesus, what was that! I whirl around toward the convoy, and then, seconds later, comes the sound of yet another explosion. Lord, more torpedoes; we've walked into a second submarine. I pass the word to the captain inside, who simply nods, too intent on our own developing attack to waste words. Moments later, *Kamsack* is diverted from us by *Montgomery*, and detailed to sweep astern for the second U-boat. The commodore reports the pennant numbers of the latest ship attacked, and corrects an earlier report; despite those first three explosions, only two ships have been torpedoed in the earlier attack—the extra bang was just one of those things.

At six hundred yards, the captain makes a bold throw-off, based on reports from the set and our plot, where the courses of target and ship have been carefully plotted. We alter thirty degrees to starboard in order to cross ahead of our unseen antagonist, so that our charges may sink through the water in his path and, hopefully, explode as he heads right to them.

Now the reports come thick and fast, the whole intensity of our effort stepping up as the range closes quickly. This is the climactic moment of the whole attack, when this ship justifies the purpose for which she was built and for which all her crew have trained and endured. The next few seconds can make it all worth while, can redeem the endless manhours and effort which ship and crew represent. Except for the chanted litany of the asdic team, intoning its bearings and ranges, there is utter silence throughout the ship, every man keyed up to the breaking point. In the asdic cabin, the black line of the echo traces will be moving along the paper tape, being aligned with the perspex firing bar; when they coincide with the etched line on the bar the firing will begin.

There it is: "Fire one!" And seconds later, "Fire two!" and then "Fire three!"

From the blackness behind us, we hear the splash of the charges from the traps into our wake, the "whoosh! whoosh!" of the throwers on each side as we drop our charges in an elongated diamond pattern of ten, with six charges in pairs on the centre line and four from the throwers, two on each side.

"Simultaneous echoes!" comes the report from the asdic operator; the target is so close that no ranging is possible, and moments later, as the target passes astern and our transmissions are blanked out by our own wake, "Lost contact, sir."

"Boom! Bang! Whoorumph!" The tremendous detonation of our charges is like a giant hammer striking our hull; the whole ship lifts and is borne aloft as a great fountain of water, sensed rather than seen, rises from astern. The ship is given a ferocious shaking, and on deck we clutch for support; in the engine room, we must have broken every pipe we have. The captain reduces speed, and we circle around to give our asdic set a clear field in which to regain contact. But in the asdic cabin there are bitter oaths; the main gyro which directs our compasses has been unseated by the explosions, and everyone works desperately to get it back in service, for without it our asdic compass is useless. The captain paces in a fury of exasperation.

How was it? we ask ourselves. In the waist, the depth-charge crews are jabbering with excitement as they reload their mortars, and all of us wait for confirmation of our success. Surely no U-boat could have survived the accurate explosion of three tons of amatol? From the plot comes confirmation that the attack seemed a good one, but still, as we circle around, comes neither contact with the U-boat nor signs of its destruction. Unless—surely that smell was not there before—surely that is the smell of oil! I call the captain out, and he sniffs excitedly, but then the smell is gone, as quickly as it came.

"Not enough for a kill; more likely she's sprung a rivet or two in her fuel tanks," the captain cautions, and moves back to the set. At long last, our gyro is operational again, and the asdic team buckles to its job. Still no contact; we begin a square search, directed by the plot, and the minutes grow, and with them our chances of regaining contact dwindle. Time is now crucial to us, for if we are not firmly in contact we cannot delay much longer. Our convoy is under attack, our escort hard-pressed, the sea perhaps covered with survivors awaiting rescue or death, men whose life in the sea is measured in minutes.

The issue we are already beginning to agonize over is resolved in a moment by a peremptory signal from *Montgomery*. We are to rejoin at best speed, and sweep astern as we do so while *Kamsack* screens the rescue ship, lying stopped

and vulnerable as she hauls shaken and sodden men from the
sea.

In dejected silence we huddle at our action stations. In an
inspired moment, somebody lays on a cup of "key" all
around, and as we sip the hot chocolate, so thick that it is
barely liquid, we fortify ourselves for the long hours of vigi-
lance which still lie ahead of us before this night is over. Our
burning motorship has disappeared, her flames presumably
snuffed out by the invading sea, and everything else has been
swept away from our world, the dark shapes of the convoy
having long vanished over the horizon ahead. We increase to
fifteen knots; it will be all we can do to regain station by
early morning.

In the event, we come up with part of the convoy earlier
than expected. At first light, the air becomes rank with a
familiar stink, and as the light grows we find ourselves steaming through a vast pool of oil, a slick of glossy slime that
seems to cover the whole ocean. It is fuel from the bunkers
of our torpedoed merchantmen, and scattered about in it is
the indescribable debris left by sunken ships. We pass
gratings, and boxes, and nameless hunks of timber, hatch-
boards, bloated canvas covers, bits of white-painted wood.
Boats, too; one of them with bows stove in and half full of
water, two others in good shape, but empty of occupants.

In silence we stare from our decks at the debris streaming
past; clusters of faces at the break of our fo'c'sle show that
even the watch below has come out to look, in shivering
silence, at these pitiful fragments from the shattered house-
holds of friends and comrades. There are worse horrors to
come; my stomach rises as I see, white in the black water, the
bloated sacs and torn flesh of what I am forced to recognize
as the lungs and viscera and abdomen of a human being, and
a little further on, a sudden pointing of arms from our onlookers below indicates a man, only his head and shoulders
visible in the filthy sea. He is dead, of course; his eyes are
open, like his twisted mouth, but he sags lifelessly against his
oil-stained lifejacket, his face as grey as the soiled canvas supporting it, his hair and cheeks plastered with the fuel oil
which has suffocated him. We steam past in awed silence; for
our first-trippers, it is a startling glimpse of the Death which
up to now has been one of war's abstractions, distant and
impersonal, something to be read about or glimpsed in a distant explosion.

Oppressed by our failure, in the bleak grey dawn we steam

through a filthy sea laden with reproach, our decks slippery with the disorder of a night action, squalid with dirty cocoa cups, blistered paint, broken glass, and fallen corking. Sullen, sleepless, and silent we rejoin HX 142.

4
THE BAND
OF BROTHERS

The real heroes of the Battle of the Atlantic were the officers and men of the Merchant Service; everyone who served at sea knows that. Even the name, "Merchant Service", was a misnomer; these men served in no organized force, wore no uniforms, earned no recognition or awards. They were civilians, and although they earned a far higher rate of pay than any naval man, no wage scale could possibly have recompensed them for the hardihood and endurance which kept them at sea, in helpless and often inadequate ships, in defiance of the terrors of the wartime North Atlantic.

But the Merchant Service made another great contribution to the winning of the Battle of the Atlantic; it provided the experienced core of men who, as Naval Reserve officers with the interwoven gold lace on their sleeves, commanded the ships of Canada's escort fleet. In the early years, every Canadian corvette was commanded by a Naval Reserve lieutenant; by the closing stages of the war a good many Volunteer Reserve officers had replaced them in corvette commands, and the more senior Naval Reserve types had gone on to take over frigates and destroyers. From first to last, though, it was the officers of the Naval Reserve, the fellows with the twisty bands of gold lace on their cuffs, who imparted a distinctive character to the seagoing Canadian fleet, an ambience quite different from that of the shoreside navy.

In the early years of the war, each corvette was a distinct and separate world, whose character reflected the personality of her captain, and whose cleanliness, discipline, and fighting capacity often varied widely from that of the sister ships alongside her.

All too often, she was a grubby, rust-streaked mess, manned by a scruffy, undisciplined crew and drunken, incompetent officers, her deplorable state reflecting the incapacity of her captain, who might be anything from a River Plater or a China Coaster to a second mate from some Great Lakes sand-sucker. I was fortunate enough to serve in clean, well-run ships commanded by capable officers, but I also served under alcoholics who used to drink up the crew's rum issue, and under thieves who used money from the ship's contingency funds for their personal expenses on a run ashore. In time, of course, the incompetents drifted off, often after running their ships ashore or running afoul of the law or of a shocked escort commander, and with their passing the seagoing navy began to shape up into an efficient and effective fleet moulded by the best of the Naval Reserve captains.

Canada was fortunate to have attracted to her navy a good number of British merchant-ship officers who had served before the war in well-run shipping lines—Canadian Pacific and Canadian National, Cunard, Royal Mail, Ellerman, British India, to name a few—or in the British-run customs and hydrographic services of China and other Asiatic countries. It was these officers, drawn to the Royal Canadian Navy on the outbreak of war by the pay, higher than that of the British Royal Navy, who not only took Canada's corvettes to sea, but imparted their rich fund of seamanship to the thousands of Volunteer Reserve officers and men who had come to sea for the first time, from Canadian schools and offices, factories and farms.

There were, of course, some memorable lapses. I was one of the group of Volunteer Reserve officers undergoing a short course to fit us to take command which was marched down to the Halifax waterfront for a lesson in ship-handling. We were in the charge of Ben Sivertz, a short, stone-faced little Icelander with the curled stripes of a Naval Reserve lieutenant on his cuffs, a piercing blue eye that never wavered, and a deliberate manner of speech; he seemed always to be speaking in capital letters. We called him "Sea-Biscuit".

He was taking us out on a little wooden-hulled auxiliary vessel, he told us, to practise bringing her alongside various wharves; presumably her light timber hull would inflict less damage on our surroundings than a conventional steel hull could be expected to do. He cautioned us to observe the manner in which the little ship's captain, an NR skipper lieutenant and formerly a Newfoundland fisherman, handled the ship. "HE MAY SEEM TO YOU A BIT ROUGH, BUT WHAT HE LACKS IN POLISH HE MORE THAN MAKES UP FOR IN HIS MASTERY OF SEAMANSHIP AND PRACTICAL SHIP-HANDLING. HE IS A MASTER OF HIS CRAFT," Sea-Biscuit intoned, and we were all suitably impressed. We watched in reverent silence while this master of the ship-handling art brought his scruffy little vessel into the berth while we waited on the jetty.

To begin with he chose to bring her in with the tide astern, instead of stemming it in the normal manner; a cardinal error, roughly equivalent to landing a light aircraft downwind in a gale. Heading into a tidal current helps to push the ship alongside its desired berth; if the ship approaches with the tide astern, the current tends to push it along parallel to the wharf. At first incredulous, then appalled, we watched as the little grey-painted ship made a lunge at the wharf before being borne irresistibly along on the tide into the sharp prows of two old destroyers secured in the berth ahead. She came to rest at right angles to the jetty, broadside on the sharp destroyer bows, and from all appearances she was there to stay for quite some time.

It was then that we were vouchsafed our first glimpse of the Master Craftsman in the flesh; a balding head, a crinkled cigarette dangling from its lower lip, was thrust out the pilot-house window; beneath it we could see the crumpled monkey-jacket, hands thrust deep in its pockets and cigarette ash down its lapels. There was no sign of alarm or distress; instead the Master sized up the situation at a glance and withdrew into the cool depths of the pilot-house. Surely, we thought, we are now about to see how a ship can be plucked from even so awkward a position as this by consummate seamanship and cunning ship-handling; we watched with bated breath.

There was this to be said for the Master Craftsman: he did not waste time with shilly-shallying, or flinch from paying the inevitable price in scraped paint and splintered wood as a more sensitive man might. He put his wheel hard over and his engines full ahead, and dragged his ship by main force across the bows of her encumbering destroyers while stanchions bent and broke, lifelines tautened bar-hard before flying apart, and great shavings of grey-painted wood were scraped from her battered sides. For a moment the bow of the innermost destroyer caught on a davit of the little ship's lifeboat, but as the propeller bit deep the davit was lifted out of its socket and parted with a screeching clangour, and the ship was free. A couple of deckhands in dirty T-shirts tossed lines onto the wharf, and the ship was made fast.

If someone had giggled, or so much as simpered, we would all have exploded with laughter, but as it happened Sea-Biscuit simply collected us with an icy glance and led us aboard over the tatty gangplank, his face a mask. We trooped dutifully aboard, and prepared to follow in the steps of the Master.

This incident, of course, was merely the exception that proved the rule; most Naval Reserve officers were fine shiphandlers.

They included some rough diamonds. One of the best of the early corvette commanders used to astound visitors to the wardroom meals by removing his false teeth for what he considered "the easy bits" and dropping them into his water-glass until they were required for masticating something more challenging. Yet another had acquired a fascinating array of tattoos during the course of long service in the Far East, and would exhibit them, in progressively more intimate areas, when plied with drink during the course of a lively wardroom evening. The pièce de résistance was a magnificent serpent, coloured in vivid shades of blue and green and scarlet, which coiled around his waist and whose head, complete with hooded eyes and scarlet tongue—but enough, enough.

Yet whatever their individual eccentricities, these ex-Merchant Service officers provided the solid core of experienced seamen on which the Canadian seagoing navy was built. It was they who shaped a force whose discipline and attitudes and standards were to prove equal to the rigorous demands of North Atlantic warfare, and which survived, to a remarkable extent, into the postwar Canadian navy.

The strain of command, particularly in the early years, was almost more than men could bear. Not only were the ships ill-armed and under-equipped, the crews inexperienced and undisciplined, the escort groups uncoordinated and ill-trained, the weather, particularly in the winter months, simply indescribable, but the shortage of escorts and the size of convoys—up to a hundred ships—imposed intolerable demands on the early corvette commanders. Each convoy trip was a test of endurance; two to three weeks of gales and sinkings and collisions, of escorts trying to take in tow huge disabled merchantmen ten times their size, of excrutiating discomfort and agonizing decisions. Sleeplessness was the rule for the corvette captains; with no other experienced officer to lean on, all decisions, night and day, were thrust on to his shoulders. In the days before oiling at sea became standard practice, fuel shortage was chronic among escorts on a long convoy run; did one risk leaving a convoy under attack to dash away for fuel, or did one remain to fight it out tonight and risk becoming a helpless hulk tomorrow?

After weeks of nightmare, a corvette would limp into Iceland, or, later on, Londonderry, for a layover of three or four days, during which the exhausted crew had to refuel, load food and ammunition for the return voyage, and attempt to repair and maintain their battered ship and armament. There was simply no time, in those early days, for proper training ashore during the brief and hectic layovers. In no time, it seemed, the ships were steaming out to sea to escort a westbound convoy, with the prospect of an equally frantic stopover in St. John's at the end of it. It was like a continuing bad dream, an endless round of misery and hardship and strain which tested officers and men, but above all, captains, to the limits of human endurance, and sometimes beyond. The wonder is, not that a few cracked under the strain, nor that hard drinking ashore during the few nights in port became a customary feature of too many commanding officers' routines, but that so many captains endured the fearsome ordeal month after month, year after year.

The aging process was fearful; who could have recognized, in the grizzled frigate captain at war's end, the feckless young second mate who had joined up only three years before?

As captains, these officers imparted their own character to the ships they commanded; a good officer ran a good ship, a poor one ran a miserable ship. You could tell them apart at a glance; a good captain ran a happy ship, a clean ship, an efficient ship. You could tell the incompetently run corvette by her slack and grubby air, by her sloppy and sullen crew, by her disordered decks. A good captain had to teach his methods and standards to his first lieutenant, had to hound him and coax him until he learned to keep his ship orderly and clean, his men content and obedient. Because experienced petty officers available for sea-duty in almost all branches were virtually non-existent, and officers and crews were green as grass to the ways of the sea, corvette captains had to concern themselves with a thousand details of ship maintenance and organization which would never concern commanding officers in peacetime warships, or even in the wartime Royal Navy, where a backbone of experienced ratings and petty officers could be depended upon to establish routines in every ship, even in emergency-program corvettes and frigates.

The key factor, to the surprise of those volunteer officers and men who looked for more martial qualities to set their ship above all others as a fighting ship, was cleanliness. With so many men crammed into a small space, sleeping and eating and operating their tiny vessel in conditions of indescribable and often chaotic discomfort, orderliness and cleanliness were absolutely essential before any sort of operational efficiency could be achieved. It was an obsessive, never-ending business; always, at sea and ashore, there were things to be cleaned—messdecks, bulkheads, washrooms—or greased—guns, winches, deck gear of every sort—or scraped and red-leaded and painted—decks and shipsides, funnels and upper-works. There was never enough time to catch up with all the work of maintaining a ship as she should be; as fast as work was done it was eroded by weather and usage. But the measure of a ship's capacity was the degree to which she was able to maintain herself, and the moment you stepped aboard a corvette you knew whether she was a happy and efficient ship or one in which even the simplest voyage would be an ordeal.

There existed a myth, particularly on the lower deck, that equated indiscipline with a happy ship, and scruffy crews of scruffy ships would excuse their shortcomings by maintaining that theirs was a "fighting ship", with no time left from battling the enemy for such frills as cleaning and painting. But the reality was quite different; cleanliness and good order spelt both contentment for the ship's company and operational efficiency. I never knew a ship which could gleam in harbour which did not also shine at sea.

Although the curly-stripers of the Naval Reserve, the ex-merchant seaman, provided the commanding officers of the new corvette navy, it was the Volunteer Reserve, the landsmen, who furnished the officers and men who manned it. Most of them had never seen the sea until they joined the navy, and their nautical experience, if any, was limited to a little freshwater yachting. In time they were to equal both merchant navy and regular navy officers as anti-submarine tacticians and corvette commanders.

This outcome was not as surprising as it might at first appear, for the tactics of U-boat warfare were as new to experienced naval officers as to the VR officers newly arrived at sea. The VR's simply gobbled up the new techniques faster than their older RCN and RCNR contemporaries, and their inexperience in the ways of sea and navy was more than counterbalanced by keenness and enthusiasm. After all, the very fact that they had chosen to go to sea in corvettes from safe and comfortable homes ashore indicated that they were anxious to give of their best, and it was this eagerness to learn which was their greatest asset. A second characteristic was a quick intelligence; some of the sharpest and brightest young men in Canada joined the new navy, and they brought to wardrooms and messdecks a feistiness which thrived on the new challenges and techniques of an ever-changing war.

But if they had certain innate virtues, the young VR officers also had certain lamentable defects, quite apart from the lack of experience which made them almost useless on early voyages. Chief among these was an almost total lack of "power of command": the ability to assume responsibility for a group of men and to impose one's will by simple, clear orders. Few Canadian VR officers in the early days had the moral courage to issue orders which they knew would not be well received; instead, too many emulated "Popularity Jack", that most despicable of officers, and attempted to curry favour with the men for whom they were responsible. Another example of this same weakness was the VR martinet, the petty tyrant who delighted in bellowing orders and extracting salutes for the sake of savouring his new-found power. Both the cringer and the strutting posturer reflected the inherent inability of most Canadians to exercise power responsibly in a service hierarchy so alien to the "democratic" institutions of Canadian civilian society.

Not the least of the contributions made by the experienced seamen of the Naval Reserve was their success in knocking this nonsense out of the VR officers who came under their command. My first corvette captain, suspecting me of "sucking up" to the signalmen on watch, told me bluntly to make up my mind whether I was to berth in the messdeck or in the wardroom, for in this ship I wasn't going to do both. At the same time, he insisted that none of his officers was to eat or sleep or go ashore until he first ensured that the men for whom he was responsible were able to do likewise, and it was this two-way lesson which made officers of young Canadian civilians.

For it was discipline which, from first to last, was the chief problem of the war-born Canadian navy. Lacking the stratified and established society of older nations, Canadians had not grown up "knowing their place", like their British counterparts, and did not take kindly to having people no better than they telling them what to do and how to do it. Saluting some fellow who'd grown up just across the street came hard to the free spirits of raw new entries, and the whole service system, hedged around with restrictions and regulations affecting their every waking moment, seemed intolerably confining to men fresh from free-and-easy civvy street. Sailors of no other nation, not even those of the United States, were so resistant to discipline as those of Canada, primarily because of the lack of seasoned petty officers, leading seamen, and commissioned officers. The combination of recalcitrant, inexperienced seamen and inadequate officers plagued the early days of the corvette navy, and was chiefly responsible for the indifferent performance of so many Canadian ships.

It took the experience of conditions at sea, of the frightening ordeal of a North Atlantic crossing, to instill in both officers and men the sense of collective identity that lies at the heart of good discipline; once it became clear that they sank or survived as a ship's company, not as individuals, the need for organized communal effort to serve a collective purpose became clear to even the most independent soul, and indiscipline ceased to be a problem. In ships blessed with good officers, particularly commanding officers, a rapport was quickly established between all ranks on board which established the vessel as that most blessed of institutions, a "happy ship". And while the standard of performance of the average Canadian ship was below that of the average British ship, particularly in the early years of the war, there was nothing afloat in the Allied navies that could touch the performance of a happy and efficient Canadian ship. In a state of good order and discipline, the Canadian sailor proved himself to be the best there was.

But he was never one to be trampled upon, as one officious commanding officer discovered to his cost. This fellow had made himself something of a martinet, and he ran afoul of the unwritten rule of seagoing etiquette that requires commanding officers to limit their strictures to their own crews. Returning to his ship one night, berthed alongside several others at a congested escort jetty, he discovered that the quartermaster of the inboard corvette was not at the gangway as he was supposed to be. In order to teach him a lesson, this pompous fellow confiscated the quartermaster's book and the small table on which it lay, and took them with him aboard his own vessel. Next morning, he sent a message to the captain of the inboard ship, an officer junior to him, notifying him that the missing articles were on board and could be reclaimed by him only, in person. The resentful fury of the humiliated captain was shared by his entire ship's company, and found expression in a revenge that became celebrated throughout the Western Approaches. That same morning the crew of the inboard ship were overside on stages and floats, touching up the paint on the bows of their vessel, and hidden from observation above by the flare of the fo'c'sle.

Next morning, the outside corvette sailed, her captain bustling importantly about his bridge—and awoke the mirth of the whole harbour. Men poured up onto the decks of ships alongside to gesture and hoot with laughter; whole ship's companies lined the rails to jeer and shriek with mirth. Ribald signals were sent to the mystified captain; drawn up on deck fore and aft, his ship's company could only wonder what all the merriment was about. It was the same when the corvette joined her convoy, long after the harbour incident had been left behind; she seemed to arouse derision wherever she went. It was not until a pointed signal from one of her fellow escorts had been received that the officious captain peered over his fo'c'sle rail to discover the full extent of his injured junior's revenge. For there, in great black letters six feet high, had been inscribed on his bows the legend: "I'M A SHIT."

A great many factors played a part in the transformation of the wartime Canadian navy from its shaky beginnings into the experienced and effective force it was to become, but the three principal elements were time, training, and—Mainguy. Time—each passing week after those first corvette commissionings in early 1941 provided experience for green crews, better armament and equipment, and more ships to build up the first puny escort groups. Training—a new Commander-in-Chief, Admiral Sir Percy Noble, emphasized training, training, and more training for the hard-pressed crews of Western Approaches escorts. Mainguy—Edmund Rollo, Captain RCN, took over as Captain D commanding the escort groups at Newfoundland and fashioned a great fighting force almost single-handed.

Looking back to the beginnings of the escort fleet, the

changes wrought upon both ships and crews by the passage of even a few months seem almost unbelievable. The first corvettes were fought from a bridge which consisted of a skimpy edge of planking fringing a glass asdic house and chart-house, protected from weather and enemy only by a painted canvas dodger and obscured from astern by the funnel top, which poured fumes over it with a following wind, and from ahead by a large foremast, which showered watch-keepers with condensation in fog, rain, or heavy dew. There was a large open gap in the main deck between bridge-house and fo'c'sle, which ensured that crew members going on and off watch, and food being brought forward from the galley, could be sure of a drenching in any head sea. Secondary armament was limited to a Lewis machine gun or two and perhaps a fellow who could throw rocks. There was no radar, no room, and not enough storage even for the depth-charges which were an escort's main armament, but there was an enormous winch and other minesweeping gear on the quarterdeck—it was thought that corvettes might double in brass as minesweepers—and an interminable wireless aerial slung between the two masts, a legacy from another still-born notion to use corvettes on the Northern Patrol between the Faeroes and Iceland. Once the true role of the corvette as ocean escort was established, changes came thick and fast. First, splinter mats were hung on the bridge railings, and a flimsy "monkey island" was improvised, by the ship's own efforts, atop the asdic house, where officers could keep watch, impeded by the direction-finding radio aerial but free from funnel smoke and the worst of the mast and rigging. Eventually, the canvas bridge dodger was replaced by wood; a spindly radar aerial, a real plumber's nightmare, snaked up the mast to serve the Canadian sw 1 c radar set, glumly viewed at the time as Hitler's Secret Weapon.

Within a year the wretched foremast had been moved aft of the bridge, where it ceased to be a curse to all; the mainmast was replaced by a stump on the pom-pom bandstand or a gaff on the funnel. A proper destroyer-type bridge had emerged, complete with windscreens and compass platform, and with asdic and chart-room space built into its leading edge. The fo'c'sle deck had been extended aft to the waist, providing both much-needed room and improved sea-keeping qualities. Armament had multiplied, with two-pounder guns (pom-poms) aft and quick-firing cannon (Oerlikons) added to the bridge wings, and depth-charges in rails and four throwers arranged on a main deck cleared of sweeping winches and gear. But best of all, radar—the reliable, efficient British 271 set—was fitted in its distinctive lantern housing above and abaft the bridge, and, with its later embellishment of repeaters in bridge and plot-room, transformed the whole technique of convoy escort.

In a matter of months the corvette was transformed into an efficient and effective warship, becoming ever more complex with each new vessel launched until it spawned, in later years, both the Castle class and, ultimately, the frigate.

The transformation wrought in a few months on the crews of Western Approaches escorts was phenomenal. To begin with, a determined effort was made to ensure that ships were given an extra day or two in harbour before turning around for the long fight back. In the early days, there was never enough time for crews to catch their breath, particularly those in the junior ships, which would always be given the dirty jobs, such as filling in for some missing escort in another group just sailing as the incoming group arrived. Most of us remember too well the terrible depression which gripped everyone on board at receiving a signal, on arrival in harbour at long last after a tough crossing, to "fuel, water, and store with all despatch", in order to catch up with some outward-bound group sailing short-handed.

As more escorts became available, such occurrences became less common; instead, an effort was made on both sides of the Atlantic to ensure that crews were given time to train, as well as repair and maintain their ships, during turn-around periods in harbour. There was individual training for gun crews, which often included a shoot at targets afloat and in the air, as the group sailed to join a convoy. Asdic teams exercised every trip in mobile "attack teachers" installed in buses at every escort port, and whole bridge teams, including captains, navigators, plotters, asdic and radar operators, signalmen, and wireless crews were tested in the marvellously sophisticated tactical tables and night action rooms.

The tactical table was a large plotting floor, where movements of model ships were plotted in accordance with actions taken by each ship's bridge team, isolated in cubbyholes all around the floor. Asdic and radar teams were given realistic contacts on their sets, signals were given, and attacks were carried out as the escort commander manoeuvred his group to cope with simulated subs; afterward, everyone trooped out to see what a shambles they'd made of things on the big plotting floor outside.

It was great fun, and marvellous training; all the situations actually met at sea could be reproduced, and for the first time a really cohesive and instinctive team reaction was developed. A set of standard group tactics was developed, most of them built around the need for illuminating the area of attack in order to spot a surfaced escaping U-boat and force him to dive, and teamwork between individual ships was developed into a fine art. It was desirable to put at least two escorts in contact with a submerged submarine, so that one could retain contact while the other attacked. Quick thinking by escort commanders in allocating precious ships to cope with attacks from several directions at once was developed on tactical tables ashore and played an increasing part in convoy battles at sea. We in the corvettes looked forward to our turn at the tables in Londonderry, St. John's, and Halifax, although we seldom emerged from the post-mortem discussions with much credit.

We were not alone in this respect. Admiral Max Horton, who took over from Noble as Commander-in-Chief of Western Approaches, was a former submarine commander who prided himself on his ability to escape from surface hunters. In an exercise at the tactical table in Liverpool, Max undertook to run the U-boat in a confrontation with a single escort. He was sunk, in short order, three successive times, and stamped out of the room in such a fit of temper that nobody had enough nerve to tell him that the "captain" of the ship which had sunk him with such ease was one of the WRNS girls who served as plotters at the unit, a little Third Officer who'd never been to sea and had been in the navy less than a year!

But the real "big time" in shore training establishments was the Night Action Room, known to one and all as Panic Incorporated. This was an enormous darkened room in which actual seagoing conditions, as well as situations, could be simulated. Every action team of a ship was closed up on bridge, guns, asdic, radar, wireless, depth-charge rails and throwers, and so on. On the bridge, it was dark as night, with a howling gale, simulated by giant fans and a pitch or roll in heavy seas as the ship altered course, and even from time to time a bucket of cold water in the face as the ship pitched into a head sea. When a gun fired, the noise was as deafening and the flash as blinding as at sea; on gun platform and quarter-

deck, crews fought their guns and depth-charges on a rolling, pitching surface in all the discomfort of wind and water
experienced at sea. The convoy could be discerned through
night glasses, or on the radar screen, just as at sea, and torpedoings, star shell, or explosions lit up the horizon in a most
realistic manner. But in Panic Incorporated everything happened at once; no sooner did one detect a submarine under
one's star shell than two ships went up in the convoy and an
urgent message was received from the escort commander,
while up a voice-pipe came the cheerful news that one's engines had broken down. After a session in the Panic room,
everyone was happy to totter off to sea for a little rest and
respite. But it was marvellous training, and it engendered a
growing confidence in the groups that they could cope with
anything.

But shore training of ships' crews was only part of the constant exercising which steadily raised the level of escort efficiency. At sea, individual ships' companies were exercised
daily at evening quarters, weather permitting; crews were
closed up at action stations before dinner, in the first dog-
watch, and tested armament and communications with a few
mock emergency drills. In the latter half of the war, escort
groups sailing out of Londonderry would be diverted to
nearby Larne, where they did intensive exercises with HMS
Philante, formerly Tom Sopwith's luxury yacht and later to
become the Norwegian royal yacht, together with a couple of
tame submarines (our own, that is).

But the really soul-testing experience, the one that every
old corvette type still recalls today with a shudder, came with
the two-week work-ups of newly commissioned ships,
designed to make a collection of odds and sods into an efficient ship's company. There were such bases at Bermuda, St.
Margaret's Bay, and Pictou on the Canadian side, but the one
that really left a lot of scar tissue was the old original, the
Dante's Inferno operated at Tobermory on the northwest
coast of Scotland by the redoubtable Vice-Admiral Gilbert
Stephenson, Royal Navy. This legendary character, variously
known as "Puggy", "The Lord of the Isles", or more com-
monly "The Old Bastard", inhabited a former passenger
steamer, *The Western Isles,* which lay at anchor in the quiet,
picturesque harbour, surrounded by a handful of newly commissioned corvettes, like a spider surrounded by the empty
husks of its victims. He was a daunting sight, smothered in
gold lace and brass buttons, with a piercing blue eye that

could open an oyster at thirty paces, and tufts of grey hair sprouting from craggy cheeks, and he preyed like some ravening dragon upon the callow crews and shaky officers served up to him at fortnightly intervals.

From dawn to dusk his signal lamp was never still. Send away both boats! Lay out a kedge anchor! Rig sheer legs and hoist in one boat! You are on fire aft! Send an armed boarding party to *Western Isles*! Prepare to take your next astern in tow! Youngest officer aboard is to take the ship to sea!

At the end of each day, an exhausted crew would tumble into their hammocks, but there was no assurance of uninterrupted slumber. On the contrary; the monster stalked its unwary prey by dark as well as by light, and seldom a night passed without an alarm of some sort. For the Admiral delighted in midnight forays; more than one commanding officer was shaken awake to find himself staring into the piercing eyes of a malevolent admiral and learn that his gangway had been left unprotected, that his ship had been taken, and that his kingdom had been given over to the Medes and the Persians.

But occasionally—just occasionally—the ships got a little of their own back. There was the occasion when the Admiral in his barge, lurking soundlessly under the fo'c'sle of what he hoped to be an unsuspecting frigate, waiting for the sailor whom he could hear humming to himself on the deck above to move on, suddenly found himself being urinated on, "from a great height", as gleeful narrators related the story in a hundred rapturous wardrooms. There was the other frigate he boarded one dark night only to be set upon by a ferocious Alsatian dog and forced to leap back into his boat, leaving, in the best comic-strip tradition, a portion of his trouser-seat aboard the ship, which ever after displayed the tattered remains as a proud trophy, suitably mounted and inscribed.

And there was the Canadian corvette sailor who worsted the fiery admiral in a hand-to-hand duel. Coming aboard this ship, the Admiral suddenly removed his cap and flung it on the deck, shouting to the astounded quartermaster: "That's an unexploded bomb; take action, quickly now!"

With surprising sang-froid, the youngster kicked the cap over the side. "Quick thinking!" commended the Admiral. Then, pointing to the slowly sinking cap, heavy with gold lace, the Admiral continued: "That's a man overboard; jump to it and save him!"

The ashen-faced matelot took one look at the icy November sea, then turned and shouted: "Man overboard! Away lifeboat's crew!"

The look on the Admiral's face, as he watched his expensive Gieves cap slowly disappear into the depths while a cursing, fumbling crew attempted to get a boat ready for lowering, was balm to the souls of all who saw it.

But if it was time that improved the ships and training that sharpened the crews, it was Captain Edmund Rollo Mainguy who imparted the spirit that fashioned Canada's escort navy into an effective and efficient team, and its officers and men into a true band of brothers, a race of men apart.

I can remember the change. We were one of a number of corvettes sent to Newfoundland in the fall of 1941 to form the Mid-Ocean Groups sailing out of St. John's, and each crossing then was a desperate effort to get our ships across as best we could, using evasive routing, often up to the limit of the Arctic pack ice, to avoid contact with U-boats, and then every kind of ruse to escape unscathed from any U-boat we encountered. Ours was a defensive effort in every way, and our object was mere survival, pure and simple. Yet by the spring of 1943 we were running convoys deliberately right at the thickest concentrations of U-boats, like a fullback running over tacklers, because this was the best way to kill as many U-boats as possible. The convoys had become bait, and our support groups, with their carriers and "hunter-killer" specialists, hung about in the offing hoping for U-boats to kill. We were on the offensive, and it was Admiral Doenitz's submariners who were now more hunted than hunter.

It was morale as well as material that made this dramatic turn-about possible, and nobody played so large a part in fashioning a winning team spirit as Mainguy, Newfoundland's Captain D.

"Newfyjohn", as the sailors called it, was a special sort of place right from the beginning; nothing like it existed anywhere else. Unlike Argentia, some miles to the south, where the Americans carved a vast and elaborate base, complete with swimming pools, out of the virgin Newfoundland forest, quite regardless of expense, the British base at St. John's was a very sketchy affair, all improvisation and make-do; more a state of mind than actual substance. Mainguy and his staff were housed on the top couple of floors of the Newfoundland Hotel, which stood on a convenient height overloking the harbour; signals were passed to ships below by signal lamp from an upper-floor window. Escorts were berthed, half a dozen deep, at the shaky jetties already standing on the South Side, across the harbour from the little city of St. John's. To this day, an old corvette type can chant their names like a sort of litany: Cashin's and Bowring's, Job's and Harvey's . . .

But whatever the base lacked in physical assets, it more than made up for in drive and energy. From the first, Mainguy oriented it and everyone who worked in it, high or low, to the service of the escort ships. This was a revolution in itself; other bases, and particularly Halifax, regarded themselves as being of primary importance and significance, with little time to spare for groups of scruffy ships and the interminable war they seemed to be involved in. But in St. John's, Mainguy insisted that the ships came first; when a corvette berthed there, battered and breathless from the fury of the Atlantic outside, staff men would be waiting on the jetty to help make good her defects, replenish her stores, and generally aid and comfort. To ships' officers accustomed, at other bases, to stand cap in hand outside office doors to await the convenience of the shore staff, this was a miracle in itself, but Mainguy did much more than that.

For one thing, his base never closed; twenty-four hours a day, seven days a week, arriving ships could be sure of full attention; none of that Halifax weekend shutdown, "try again tomorrow", sort of nonsense in Newfyjohn. But above all, Mainguy was the first Canadian Captain D to concern himself with the men as well as the ships they sailed, with morale as well as material needs.

We had been based at Halifax before Newfoundland became operational, and were accustomed, on arrival from sea, to be treated as a pestilential nuisance. Halifax Port Orders, like the Ten Commandments, were heavy on "Thou shalt not", and the negative was emphasized throughout in base attitudes to us. We were not to dump garbage overside, we were not to appear out of full uniform, we were not to go beyond this street or into that area, we were not to interfere with this or that or the other thing, and, as an appropriately repressive finale, we were required to land an armed sentry on the jetty whose function, we inferred, was not so much to defend our ships as to protect the shore from our licentious and unruly seamen.

Newfyjohn was a different world; as you arrived in harbour a signal lamp would flash you, along with berthing instructions, news of the night's dance or concert party. For the men, Mainguy established a rest camp where an exhausted crew could forget the sea in a lovely woodland setting, living in tents and huts and busying themselves with baseball and fishing and swimming, the forgotten recreations of civvy street. There were dances and shows and parties of one sort or another every night in the Caribou Hut or the Knights of Columbus Hall or elsewhere, especially laid on for the fellows from the ships, and the Salvation Army had something going every day for the sailor home from the sea.

For ships' officers Mainguy obtained the loan of the fourth floor of an old Water Street warehouse; working parties of ships' officers cleaned it up, rigged a bar and a fireplace, and inaugurated the Seagoing Officers Club. With its fifty-nine steps up a spidery outside staircase, its crest-covered walls— each ship, on arrival, was required to design and furnish an appropriate ship's crest if it did not already have one—the club became famous throughout Western Approaches as The Crowsnest, where you could forgather with friends from other ships, free from the starchiness of shoreside messes, and where women were admitted, Tuesday nights only, on condition "that they did not clutter up the bar". Mainguy himself used to preside every Saturday afternoon at his celebrated cocktail party in the Newfoundland Hotel; "Captain D's cocktail party" became a social highlight of the escort officers' routine as enjoyable, in a different way, as the raffish Saturday night "Rat Race" at the Nova Scotian Hotel in Halifax.

But more than anything else, Mainguy instilled a sense of team spirit, of pride in one's ship and in one's escort group. He did it by fostering inter-ship and inter-group competition in every sport and pastime imaginable: softball, swimming races, rowing races, even huge tug-of-war matches, involving half a ship's company against half another crew, on the jetty alongside their ships. Such tug-of-war competitions, often in winter snow, with literally hundreds of men involved and with many hundreds more watching from crowded ships alongside, had to be seen to be appreciated. Enormous and complicated wagers were made between ship and ship, mess and mess, wardroom and wardroom; indeed, the paying off of the wagers was in itself a recurring spectacle at the escort berths.

A ship sailing out of Newfy quickly became a proud ship: proud of itself, of its group, of the Western Approaches escort force. We were by no means all Canadian; British, Free

French, Polish, and Norwegian ships were among us, sometimes as distinct groups, more often mixed in with ships of
other nationalities. Ships would be moved from one escort
group to another, on occasion, and it was commonplace for a
Canadian group to have a British senior officer, particularly
in the early years when Canadians were short of destroyers.
Little by little, each group evolved a distinct identity, usually
reflecting the personality of its senior officer. There were serious groups and light-hearted ones, and ships were proud to
show their affiliation by distinctive group flags, songs, and
funnel markings.

Most of the early Canadian groups were known by the
nicknames of the veteran River-class destroyers which carried
their senior officer. There was the "Guts", or "Rustyguts", for
Restigouche; the "Sally", or "Sally Rand", for *Saint Laurent*;
the "Bones" for *Assiniboine*; the "Sag" for *Saguenay*; and so
on. Over the years we sailed with most of them, and for our
money the "Sally", when she was commanded by that austere, black-bearded patriarch Herbert Rayner, Commander
RCN, was far and away the finest senior ship to sail with we
ever knew. But the best-known was probably the Canadian escort group known as the Barber-Pole Brigade, variously led
by *Ottawa* and *Skeena* over the years, with their distinctive
barber-pole funnel stripping and their famous song, written
by *Skeena*'s medical officer.

Perhaps nothing else is more redolent of the wartime ca-
maraderie and team spirit of the old western ocean escort
days than the Barber-Pole song, sung with rousing verve to
the tune of "The Road to the Isles":

It's away! Outward, the swinging fo'c'sles reel,
From the smoking sea's white glare upon the strand;
It's the grey seas that are shipping under keel,
When we're rolling outward bound from Newfoundland!

Chorus (much waving of glasses):
From Halifax to Newfyjohn or Derry's clustered towers,
By trackless paths where conning towers roll;
If you know another group in which you'd rather spend your hours,
You've never sailed beneath the Barber Pole!

5
THE CHARACTERS

~~~~~~

The big wardroom at HMCS *Halo*, formerly the clubhouse of
the Pictou golf club, was warm and crowded; the undertone
of conversation was still subdued but becoming more animated as the crowd of officers and guests steadily increased.
The officers of the training base were playing host to a very
important guest on this summer Saturday afternoon, none
other than Captain D himself, come all the way from Halifax
on an official visit of inspection, and the base commander
had pulled out all the stops to do him suitable honour.

In addition to officers of the establishment and their wives,
all that was fairest and best in nearby Pictou had been in-
vited to take part in the festivities, "and bright the lamps
shone over fair women and brave men."

To grace the occasion, some of the magnificent wardroom
silver had been brought down from the officers' mess at HMCS
Stadacona in Halifax; in the centre of the room a tremendous
silver punchbowl, alive with mermaids and porpoises and
Neptune himself, dominated a table laden with flowers and
crystal and snowy linen. The guests were animated but deco-
rous, awaiting the arrival of the great man, who was expected
at any moment.

Attention was suddenly drawn to the entry of a slim VR
lieutenant. It was not so much the officer himself who drew
the eye, but rather the expression of stern resolve on his pale
features; here was a man, it was clear, who had some fixed
purpose in mind and was determined on its execution, whatever the obstacles, whatever the cost.

After a moment's hesitation on the threshold, the young officer fixed his eyes on the central table. The die had obviously

been cast, and his course now lay clear before him. With quick, purposeful steps he crossed the polished floor and stood before the massive punchbowl, which was flanked by a glittering mountain of glasses and vases and gladioli.

Tony "Tiger" Turner, for it was indeed none other, drew himself to attention with the exaggerated solemnity of the performer. Every eye was now upon him, and in the sudden hush one could sense the instinctive awareness of everyone present that they were about to witness something out of the ordinary, something really memorable. There was a snap and precision about the young officer's every movement which held the attention of the most casual, while in the minds of those who knew him, a sense of impending disaster paralysed the will. In mingled wonder and fascination, the distinguished gathering watched the performance now unfolding in its midst.

And what a performance it was! Staring straight before him, body erect and heels together, Turner placed a hand, palm downward, on the immaculate linen cloth on either side of the brimming silver bowl. He rose, poised, to the balls of his feet, paused, and then with a little cry, such as circus performers give, he sprang into the air, feet pointing ceilingward, supporting his weight on his arms. For an instant, he fought for control, then, gaining full balance, he stood inverted in a perfect armstand on the table, a magnificent living centrepiece.

There was not so much as a breath in the enraptured audience, as Turner, fighting to maintain control, slowly bent his elbows to lower his head into the punch and into the classic perfection of the headstand. Down, down went his curly head; up, up rose the iced pink of the punch, until it brimmed the bowl, lapped over onto the snowy white of the linen cloth. For just an instant—an instant that will live forever in the minds of all who beheld it—Turner held the full headstand. Then, like some mighty forest giant at the moment of its fall, the figure wavered, began to sway, to move, to topple.

God! What a fall was there—In one magnificent, mindboggling crash, Turner, glasses, vases, flowers, punchbowl, cloth, and table smashed to the floor in a tidal wave of pink punch, and inundation that engulfed and swept away all pretensions and inhibitions. The party that ensued, and into which a startled Captain D was swept on his arrival a few moments later, was of truly heroic proportions; nor was it in any way diminished when the founder of the festivities was discovered asleep an hour or two later, reclining at length, in full uniform, in a bath half-filled with tepid water. He had been ill.

Tiger Turner's headstand was widely celebrated in the wardrooms and messdecks of the corvette navy, but it was only one of the feats and triumphs of a band of characters who added such savour to life in the North Atlantic escort ships. Indeed, it is of these characters and their doings that old corvette types like to reminisce, at rare moments of re-union, long after serious aspects of the war at sea have been forgotten. It's not of admirals or achievements one likes to gossip, but rather of Harry the Horse, Pavillard, the "Mad Spaniard", Foghorn Davis, Two-Gun Ryan—

Was there ever such a centre of gleeful stories as Two-Gun Ryan?

Two-Gun—the origins of this nickname are lost in antiquity, but he was so known to everyone, everywhere, of high and low estate—had had a colourful and adventurous past long before he came to the Canadian navy in the Second World War. As a young officer in the Royal Navy, he had taken part in minesweeping operations in Russian waters in the ill-fated White Russian campaign against the Communists at the close of the First World War, and had been decorated for his services. After leaving the navy, he drifted into the Black and Tans, the para-military police force so execrated by Irish nationalists, and after a brief service in Ireland he turned up in New York. Making the most of his minor medal, his English accent, and his shadowy service in Ireland, he presented himself as a former undercover officer of Scotland Yard, decorated for various hush-hush missions in the service of the state, and on the strength of this he secured employment in private security work, eventually launching out on his own. When war broke out, he came to Canada, and because of his RN service twenty years before, he was commissioned as a regular-service officer with enormous seniority as a lieutenant-commander, later rising to commander.

For his superior officers, life became an endless problem of what to do with Ryan; he was perpetually in hot water, but his seniority had to be respected.

Two-Gun was a swashbuckler of enormous panache, blessed with outrageous gall, and with a disregard for the pretensions of authority which won him instant fame in the escort fleet. Once, when the Canadian destroyer in which he was serving was berthed alongside HMS *Vulcan,* the British depot ship in Iceland, an immaculate Royal Navy lieutenant, carrying his brass officer-of-the-watch telescope under his arm, came aboard to complain, in plummy upper-class accents, that smoke from the Canadian ship's funnels was fouling *Vulcan*'s pristine paintwork.

Ryan's response was instantaneous. Sending for the enormous range-finder telescope mounted in the ship's gunnery director tower and girding himself with a borrowed sword, he hastened aboard the British vessel. Sword clanking on the deck from his sagging belt, and with a prodigious six-foot telescope clutched precariously under one arm, supported at each end by the smallest ratings he could find, he presented his compliments to the plummy-voiced paragon. He then begged leave to lodge a complaint against *Vulcan*'s officers, who were in the habit of smoking and dropping their cigarette ash overside, thus befouling his destroyer's immaculate decks.

Two-Gun's career in command was brief but dramatic. As a result of the sudden illness of his captain, Two-Gun was put in charge of his destroyer for a convoy crossing, and instantly assumed the airs and honours of a very senior officer indeed. Arriving to join his convoy, he found it already under escort by the British group which Two-Gun's destroyer was instructed to join, and he proceeded to flash stationing instructions to the nearest British corvette. Stung by this assumption of authority by a Canadian interloper, the British escort commander at the head of the convoy asserted his seniority to Ryan and instructed him to take up a subordinate position on the screen. This did not sit well with Two-Gun; he would brook no ordering about by some RN puppy half his age. Firing off a signal to the senior officer, informing him that serious engine defects compelled immediate return to harbour, he cranked up to full speed and charged off homeward.

In response to an infuriated signal, ordering him to return to the convoy forthwith, Two-Gun, as he disappeared over the horizon, sent a blithe farewell: "Good-bye and good hunting!"

It cost him his command, of course, but in a rare moment of inspiration some appointment officer ashore found the ideal spot for Two-Gun. He was appointed technical advisor for a navy film being made by John Huston, and arrived in Hollywood, where he found himself in his element. He spent a good deal of the war there, starlets on each arm, cutting a dash as the swashbuckling wartime naval hero, full of salty stories of derring-do.

Unfortunately, even a Hollywood epic eventually gets completed, and Ryan then found himself out of a job. A desperate appointments officer, clutching at any straw, next sent him to act "in an advisory capacity" to a group of West Coast minesweepers being sent around from Equimalt to Halifax, via the Panama Canal. Ryan's wide acquaintance on the California coast, it was piously hoped, might prove useful to the little flotilla.

Useful was an understatement; the flotilla arrived at San Pedro, the port of Los Angeles, and, with Ryan as master of the Revels, settled down to the time of their lives.

Day followed festive day; the flotilla would have been there yet if indignant naval authority had not routed out the Canadian consulate and bundled the ships back to sea.

After passing through the Panama Canal, Two-Gun, who had by now appointed himself senior officer of the flotilla, with the eager acquiescence of all concerned, headed for the Caribbean, and the flesh-pots of Jamaica. Once arrived, the flotilla virtually disappeared so far as Canadian naval authorities were concerned; Two-Gun had settled in for a long stay and with the Glass Bucket, the Ligunae Club, and the Myrtle Bank under his lee, and with rum punches and sun and surf and rafts of lonely Wrens close to hand, no amount of signalled spleen from the Canadian snows was going to prise the ships out of Kingston harbour.

Eventually, an outraged headquarters was forced to send a senior officer to Jamaica to take over command of the flotilla and restore it to its duty. A chastened Two-Gun trailed back to Canada, and it was there that his naval service was abruptly terminated, thus bringing to an end a saga of glorious misadventure that still lives in the memory of old corvette types.

I have had the privilege myself of sailing with a few notable characters. One such was known to one and all as Sam, although this was not his Christian name. There was a craze for Damon Runyon in our group at this time, and our shipmate had been dubbed Sam the Goniff after one of Runyon's Broadway characters.

A delightful shipmate, Sam was the hero of a dozen notable adventures; he was born to trouble as the sparks fly upward. For one thing, when inflamed with the grape he had a tendency to overestimate his pugilistic prowess, and this cost him heavily, more than once. On one occasion, escorting a lady home from Captain D's cocktail party, he took exception to some coarse jests passed by a gang of toughs lounging around a Water Street lamp-post.

Their remarks, he told them, were an insult to the lady he was escorting; once he had seen her home, he proposed to return and teach them a lesson that would make finer, better-spoken men of them all. And by George, if he didn't attempt to do just that; depositing the lady at her home, he returned to the scene of his encounter, and to an astounded gang of roughs who could scarcely believe their good fortune. They were willing workers, however, and quickly fell to the congenial task of thrashing him, with fist and boot, to within an inch of his life.

This strain of physical abuse seemed to run, like a dark thread, through most of Sam's misadventures; no man shed more blood in the service than he. But his greatest moment was undoubtedly the dark night when, returning to the ship from an eventful run ashore, he missed his footing in stepping across to our fo'c'sle from the ship inboard of us, and fell between the two vessels.

He hit the water immediately opposite the open porthole of the first lieutenant's cabin on the inboard ship; a small tidal wave of oily water slopped over the port and splashed onto the face of Bill Ferguson, sleeping the sleep of the just in his berth below. Starting up in the pitch-black cabin, still only half awake, Bill realized where the water had come from and slammed the portlight shut, clamping it down to keep out any more waves, and promptly relapsed into slumber.

Angered by such a callous response, Sam pressed his face against the scuttle, shouting at the top of his voice and beating with his free fist against the steel ship's side. Alarmed and puzzled by this outcry, Bill sat up in his berth, switched on the light, and, turning toward the porthole, beheld a sight which he later maintained he would bear with him to the grave. Pressed against the streaked glass was a demonic face, its features writhing in the grip of some powerful passion, its black beard soaked and snakelike, its mouth snarling some fearful threat, inaudible through the thick glass. It was as though some demon of the deep struggled without, thirsting for his blood, and yet there was something vaguely familiar about those contorted features, those knotted whiskers—

It was a shaken, white-faced Ferguson who, moments later, assisted the quartermasters of the two ships to hoist a sodden, swearing Sam up and inboard. Restored to his own deck, Sam trailed off below without another word, his soaked cap hanging limply over his ears, leaving a little trail of oily water and the occasional orange peel behind him on the deck. It had been a full evening.

Jimmy Davis must surely have been one of the best-known, and certainly the best-liked, of all the officers of the escort fleet. With a face like a torn boot and a voice like a bull's bellow, he was everywhere known affectionately as "Foghorn Davis", and his inspired whimsy gave rise to some of the most cherished anecdotes of the ocean war. Like the Norse sagas, which they somewhat resembled, they tended to become embroidered and amended by legend, so that some of the details came to blur a bit with the passage of time, but the gist of them has survived innumerable re-tellings. Because his first command, the Fairmile motor launch Q 60, had been built in Orillia, the "Mariposa" of the celebrated Leacock *Sunshine Sketches,* he christened her *The Mariposa Belle.* Determined to make the most of his commanding officer status, even in so tiny a vessel, he had the four stripes of a full captain stitched onto a pyjama jacket he wore at sea, along with a row of bottle tops fastened, like service stars, across his manly chest.

He cut an even greater dash as a corvette captain; once, backing out from his berth and finding it awkward to turn his ship around in a busy Halifax harbour, he took her to sea stern first. The spectacle of his ship, with all hands correctly fallen in and standing to attention on fo'c'sle and quarterdeck while he saluted the Admiral, brought crowds of astounded onlookers to line the jetties and decks of ships alongside; sure enough, there was Foghorn Davis going to sea arse-end first, piping the Admiral in proper seamanlike fashion as his ship slid by at increasing speed.

Once, on a Christmas afternoon at sea, fellow members of the escort group were astounded to see Foghorn close to the convoy, bringing up alongside a big troop-carrying liner in the centre column. Through their glasses they could see the big ship's decks lined with troops, all eagerly looking outboard; faintly over the water came the sound of music and delighted cheering. Closer scrutiny revealed the cause of all the merriment: on his fo'c'sle deck, to the accompaniment of music blared over the ship's loud hailer, Foghorn was putting on a regular revue, with a chorus line of husky seaman, in brief skirts and elaborate head-dresses and the biggest false bosoms ever seen on land or sea. Foghorn's Christmas show for a shipload of delighted troops bound overseas became an established part of the Davis legend.

But equally famous was the anecdote of the earrings. During a run ashore in one of the escort ports with a fellow corvette type—was it *Calgary*'s skipper Hank Hill?—Foghorn is supposed to have conceived the notion that a small gold earring, such as Drake's sea-dogs used to wear and such are still seen in the ears of seamen in the Portuguese fishing fleet, would add a certain salty swagger. Accordingly, the two each had an ear pierced and wore in it a tiny gold ring, to the immediate consternation of their fellow-officers. But consternation gave way in time to secret admiration, then emulation; in no time, small gold rings began to appear in the two ships' companies.

It all came to an end one night when Foghorn was returning to his ship. The sentry who saluted him on the jetty, he noted, was wearing a gold earring. The quartermaster who met him at the gangway was wearing an earring, too, and so, he noticed, was every one of the group of returning libertymen just ahead of him. But the final straw came as he made his way along the deck; there, outside the galley, was the ship's cat, and in its ear was a small, glittering ring.

"That does it!" bellowed Foghorn, reaching for his ear. "Off they all come!"

But while Foghorn Davis was the hero of a dozen stories, lesser men had to be content to be associated with some single episode in the folklore of the corvette navy. Johnny Poulson, for example, is always remembered for his famous demonstration of football tackling, Canadian style. Poulson, a notable athlete, was discussing with a British contemporary in a Greenock pub the principles of good ankle tackling, as executed by a top Canadian outside wing like Wes Cutler, for example, compared with the clutch-and-grab method all too prevalent in British rugger. The argument that ensued continued after closing time, as the two made their way through the now-deserted streets toward the escort berths. As they turned into the top of the last street along their route, they encountered a milkman making his early-morning rounds, with a metal basket full of clanking bottles under each arm and his wagon following on behind, pulled by a large, somnolent horse.

"The idea behind our sort of ankle-tackling," continued Poulson, "is to knock the feet cleanly out from under, thus letting the victim's own weight and the law of gravity do all the work of bringing him down. Minimum effort for maximum effect."

As they made their way down, Poulson's eye was drawn to the milkman across the street, who was proceeding in the opposite direction complete with baskets, bottles, wagon, and horse. With sudden interest he measured the closing gap between them with a speculative eye. In an instant the fateful decision was made: now! Now was the time!

"Watch this!" he said, unbuttoning his jacket and handing it, together with his cap, to his astounded friend. Before any protest could be made, he was off; his friend could only watch, aghast, as the burly figure of the Canadian flew across the street and bore down upon the unsuspecting milkman, with his fragile load and plodding horse. Powerless to intervene, the sole spectator could only shout a warning to the intended victim, his mind reeling from the prospect of the coming collision, with its inevitable aftermath of broken glass and spilled milk.

Straight as an arrow the big Canadian flew until, nearing his quarry, he bent forward and launched himself, outstretched parallel to the ground, with all his force and weight directed the ankles of his hapless victim.

There was a crunching impact, clearly audible to the stunned spectator on the other side of the street, and then the bulging horse, watched by its astounded master, toppled backwards into a sitting position with a look of pained surprise on its long face, and with the legs of its tackler projecting from beneath its massive backside.

"Poulson's tackle" became a legend; the price of such immortality was three broken ribs.

Some characters are remembered for a word, a remark; "Pappy" Old was such a one. Back from an interlude on the Aruba oil run in the Caribbean, Pappy endeavoured to bring his corvette alongside ours with the tide, instead of stemming it, not an easy feat with a single-screw ship at an awkward berth. Pappy, a delightful, diminutive little man with a round, pink face, peered anxiously over the bridge dodger as his ship bore down on us at an alarming rate of knots; his first lieutenant, Jim Elmsley, a friend of mine, collected large numbers of men with fenders on the fo'c'sle for what he considered the inevitable catastrophe.

What followed had the quality of an endless, repetitive nightmare. The ship came to rest with stern sticking out and her bows riding over our fo'c'sle, grinding stanchions against anchors and rivets. Pappy would nip up and peek anxiously at the scene of carnage below him, then bob down to pass an order down the voice-pipe. He would go astern, and his bows would drag and grind along ours, to the accompaniment of twanging and crunches, while Elmsley and I, each on our own fo'c'sle, leaped about with fender parties.

A moon face, pink and worried, over the dodger: "Slow ahead." Twang! Bang! Boom! Crunch! Screech! Again the pink moon: "Slow astern." Screech! Crunch! Boom! Bang! Twang!

Minute after agonizing minute, Pappy's corvette sawed away at ours, while Elmsley sucked his teeth reprovingly and his anchor played hopscotch with our fo'c'sle railing.

In the middle of this ghastly performance, Pappy popped his head over the bridge and uttered his deathless remark: "You know, Number One," he said, addressing Elmsley, "I never should have tried this."

Ever after, even to this day, when landed in the soup on the golf course, in the office, or at home by an over-confident move, one can hear this classic remark from an old corvette type. There were many such situations in the corvette navy, and Pappy Old's remark was so apt that it was instantly caught up, and its creator became an overnight "character" on the strength of it.

Ivan Edwards was a character, too, but of a unique kind. He must surely have been the best-loved man in the navy, and certainly one of the few padres in the service still remembered. Protestant clergymen in the navy were generally a poor lot, either callow kids fresh out of college or failures unable to secure a good church ashore. The Salvation Army and the Roman Catholics did much better; they sent us keen young men of ability and understanding, and won trust and respect thereby. But the rest were a nondescript lot, incapable of comprehending the traumatic spiritual and mental experience of corvette crews in a North Atlantic winter. They would approach a harried first lieutenant in the middle of a hectic working morning with a request to "have a word with the lads", then loaf about the wardroom to cadge drinks and lunch.

Edwards was the opposite of these tiresome nuisances. An impressive fellow physically, he had been a first-class football player at college and in the Big Four, and he was tireless in organizing games and relaxation for cramped corvette crews.

But it was his sympathy and understanding of what these kids were going through, thrust from sheltered homes into a harsh, uncaring ocean as remote and elemental as outer space, where every treasured human value counted for less than nothing, where reason reeled and faith was tested to its utter limits; it was his instinctive comprehension of the gulf that separated lonely sea from comfortable shore that made Edwards unique. He was truly a Christian, and a delightful fellow to boot, destined, alas, to die before his time.

Like most men of the cloth, he had a relish for jokes with a clerical flavor, and it was he who first told us the joke that was later to become famous. The Protestant husband in a mixed marriage, it seems, was being taken by his Catholic wife to her church for the first time, and was nervous about the unfamiliar protocol. "There's no need to worry," she reassured him. "Just watch me closely, and do what I do."

Sure enough, things went swimmingly; the husband had no trouble in conforming to his wife's lead. Until, that is, he kneeled a little too far forward, and the hassock on which he intended to rest his knees slid backward, coming to rest between his shins. As the prayer went on he became uncomfortable kneeling on the hard floor, and reaching furtively between his legs, he groped for the hassock behind him. His squirmings distracted his wife, who hissed in an irritated whisper:

"What's the matter? Is your fly undone?"

"No," responded the husband, and then, as the thought struck him: "Ought it to be?"

Some people became characters because of a nickname— one of the founding fathers of the Volunteer Reserve was known affectionately to everyone as "Useless Eustace"—a disability, an affectation. Chummy Prentice was famous for the monocle screwed into his eye, but Ted Orde's eye was as celebrated as Nelson's. (You could always win a drink on the strength of Nelson's eye. He wore a green shade over his good left eye to shield it from strong light, not over the sightless right one.) Ted Orde had a glass eye, and at parties he would turn up with a supply of spare eyeballs in his pocket. As the evening progressed, he would pop in a replacement from time to time, each one successively more bloodshot, supposedly, he claimed, to match the progress of his good eye. At the climax of the evening, he would pop in an eyeball which had a bright Union Jack on its pupil, a spectacle so shattering as to cause women to faint and strong men to turn pale.

Not all the corvette "characters" were funny fellows; there were some nasty ones, and some tragic characters, as well. I was shipmate in one of the early corvettes with an intelligent, sensitive, high-spirited fellow, with an infallible flair for landing himself, and all about him, in trouble of one sort or another. He was the sort who would miss the last train back, who'd oversleep an early sailing, who'd discover, a thousand miles from friends, that he'd left his wallet on his bureau. A terrific fellow to be at a party with, as I used to tell myself when I'd haul him up from under the table at the Old Colony Club and half carry him outside. Once in the frosty air, he'd bounce up, all bright-eyed and sober, only to do an el foldo back in the warmth inside.

He missed a sailing once, and we were short-handed on a long convoy crossing over and back; everyone was furious at him. The captain thought he needed a better influence than the rest of us were providing, and was glad to see, on our return to Newfyjohn, that our boy had made friends with the bright young priest who'd just been assigned padre to the groups. Two nights later the priest, well sozzled, together with our friend, also brightly illuminated, drove an expensive automobile, not his own, into the harbour, whence the two—but not the car—were extricated by the gendarmes. The young priest was banished in disgrace to some clerical Siberia, and we had to leave our boy behind to face another court—an experience with which we became increasingly familiar.

After a reprimand, and a loss of seniority, he was posted to another ship, only to repeat the performance; a great fellow to have around at sea, but totally irresponsible when he was on the old juice, which was just about every time he was ashore. We'd hear of his escapades from time to time: how he'd lost all his uniform except a pair of trousers in Boston, and then, more serious, how he'd missed his ship again.

It was the last straw. A friend, staying at the Admiralty House for a course, told of meeting him there.

"What, here for a course?" he had inquired brightly. "I'm here for a court"

That was to be the last of all the gaiety that endeared him to us all. On New Year's Eve in the mess, with the sounds of merriment all about him, he had gone upstairs to the washroom. There, in some private purgatory of his own, this bright, erratic, and lovable youth, only a few months before peace would make a joke of all his troubles, blew out his brains; a crueller tragedy to all of us who knew him than the deaths of any who went down with their ships.

6
PORTS OF CALL

~~~~~~

Esquimalt—Squiggley, the matelots called it—the lonely landlocked harbour just outside Victoria, B.C., was the first naval base we had seen, and we arrived there for gunnery training early enough to enjoy it in its peacetime innocence. Japan had not yet entered the war and the Pacific was just that, thousands of miles away from the Battle of the Atlantic. With its low, galleried brick barrack buildings enclosing the upper parade ground, its polished brass, its white-painted perimeters, its flowers and tennis courts and aura of sunlit serenity, Esquimalt's naval base, HMCS *Naden,* was a delightful relic of the Edwardian Royal Navy that had somehow survived, like a living fossil, into another age, another continent. Its wardroom had collected some of the most incredible eccentrics to be found anywhere. I still remember the introduction of a new chaplain dining in the mess for the first time, who was asked to say grace by the presiding senior officer, a red-faced Royal Navy type brought back out of retirement, and grudging every moment of his service.

"For what we are about to receive," muttered the padre, as we sat with bowed head, "thank God." It was the traditional naval grace, brief and to the point, we thought, but it seemed to infuriate the presiding officer. Hurling down his napkin, his face an even brighter scarlet and his neck bulging with rage, he bellowed: "By God, padre, we'll have none of your papist nonsense in this mess! A simple 'Thank God!' will suffice!"

It was an appropriate introduction to a collection of retired RN types, of former China Coasters and assorted characters as colourful as any we were ever to find anywhere; as very

75

junior VR sublieutenants, the lowest form of animal life, we tiptoed about the place and did our best to keep out of the way of all these choleric, hard-drinking characters who seemed to be in perpetual dudgeon, and endowed with vocabularies that opened ever new and more fearful horizons to our innocent ears. They included a mean, black-visaged type reputed to be a black-belt judo expert, a good man to keep clear of. We were to run into him later as a corvette commander in the Atlantic, where he was to go off his head and have to be locked, shrieking, in his cabin. There was the moon-faced retired lieutenant with the medal of the Victoria Cross on his chest, the only one we ever saw. He viewed the world through thick, frog-like glasses from the depths of his leather chair, and was reputed to have taken a motor-launch into Zeebrugge, after everyone else had left in the famous First World War raid, and brought away a lot of stranded big brass through a hail of lead. Nowadays he put away a bottle of Scotch a day. There was the old submariner who, glass in one hand, was perpetually wriggling the other about to demonstrate how he would slip away and evade the furious attacks of brother officers, all keen and determined submarine slayers. There was the crusty old gunnery type, whose ancient black leather gaiters and tiny Jellicoe cap were right out of a Victorian Whale Island, as were his muttered parade-ground asides, picked up by the newfangled loudspeaker microphones and made audible to a startled and astounded ship's company daily at morning divisions. But above all there was Commander Kingscote, base executive officer and the presiding genius of the place, surely the most delightful officer and finest gentleman to ever grace the naval service. A tall, rangy figure, with a craggy face and bushy, beetling brows, he had been a champion boxer in his day, and looked as if he could still handle anyone who came his way, but he had a warm heart, a ready sympathy, and a quick understanding, as well as a sunny disposition and a salty sense of humour. We all loved him, and would cheerfully have died for him; lacking suitable occasion, however, we carried kelp for him from the harbour edge to his garden on Saturday afternoons, and were rewarded afterward with tea in his pleasant home. Kingscote was the finest officer we ever met, a credit to Britain where he was born and to the Royal Navy which moulded him, and everyone, officer and man, who ever passed through *Naden* cherishes his memories of him.

Our West Coast service was a sort of idyllic interlude in a grim wartime period; a kind of never-never land where the most curious things seemed to happen. Being all dead keen, we made the most of every emergency. Like the day the boom-defence scow caught fire, and we volunteered for the fire-fighting party that went swooshing off, at a great rate of knots, to the little vessel lying in a cloud of smoke in the harbour entrance. Will we ever forget rushing around a corner of the narrow deck and coming face to face with a livid Commodore Brodeur, Commanding Officer, Pacific Coast, and ranked second on the Pacific only to God Himself, with his foot in a bucket of grey paint and filling the air with guttural French-Canadian curses!

Apparently Vic (as we called him behind his back) had decided to liven the boredom of an Esquimalt weekend by dashing off in his barge to oversee the firefighting efforts in person. He'd come hurrying around a corner and put his foot right into the open pot of paint some crewman had been using a few moments before. The spectacle of the Commodore shaking the pot from his foot and, without a backward look, getting stiffly down into his boat in a splatter of battleship grey we shall carry gratefully to our grave.

And who will ever forget the furious aerial sneak attack on the tugboat *Haro*, a day of infamy second only to Pearl Harbor? One Saturday morning we'd all been loaded aboard the *Sans Peur*, formerly the Duke of Sutherland's yacht and the largest warship we had at Squiggley, and had dashed off to sea, where we cruised up and down off William Head, with all guns crews closed up and lookouts eagerly searching the sky. It seemed there was to be a combined air-sea operation; the air force were sending over some planes to practise dive-bombing on us while our gunners practised laying and training on fast-moving aircraft. Minutes ticked by, lenghtening into hours; after tracking seagulls in their sights for a few minutes, even the keenest gunners grew weary, and relapsed into sullen, tooth-sucking silence. Finally, at eleven o'clock, it was clear to all there'd been a hitch somewhere and the air force were not going to put in an appearance; cranking up to full speed, we hustled back to harbour in time for afternoon make-and-mend, and the harbour entrance relapsed into its usual weekend somnolence.

The only sign of life, if it can be called that, was the ancient steam tug *Haro*, drifting on station as examination vessel at the port approaches. A solitary seaman on watch sat in a chair propped against the wheelhouse and picked his teeth in the sunshine; everyone else was below taking things easy.

An angry sound disturbed the noonday silence, grew louder, closer. Glancing skyward, the *Haro*'s watch-keeper caught sight of a handful of aircraft, flying high in tight formation; he watched with idle interest as they approached, opened out, began to circle overhead.

The air force, as usual, had arrived late; had someone mis-read the appointed time? In any case they had arrived for their exercise, loaded for bear, or at least with bags of flour for their dive-bombing markers. A ship, to these air-force types, was a ship, and there below them, in the designated area, was a ship, the only one in sight. The leading aircraft peeled off and screeched down in a shrieking dive, straight at the hapless *Haro*.

With wondering disbelief the *Haro*'s watch-keeper watched the plane hurl its flour bag straight at him, then pull up, only feet above the mast, and go screaming off, level with the far horizon. The bag burst squarely on the bows of the sleeping tugboat; in an instant its wheelhouse, its tarry deck, its whole forepart were covered in snowy white. The impact brought every crewman to the open doors and scuttles of the poor old *Haro*; in silent wonder they stood gaping while plane after plane came swooping down on them, sending bags of flour hurtling into the sea about them, or bursting on decks and upper-works. To the dumbfounded crewmen, it was as if the world had gone suddenly mad, a meaningless maelstrom of snarling planes and bursting bags, wrapped in clouds of swirling white.

The nightmare ended as quickly as it had begun; suddenly, all was silent again, and the dazed crew could take stock of the old *Haro*, now converted into a white ghost of herself, like some old spectral turtle. Squiggley's "Pearl Harbor" was over.

Not the least of *Naden*'s assets was a rich collection of colourful petty officers, nearly all of them long retired from the Royal Navy's Eastern Fleet and China Station, back do-ing their bit by shaping up this new lot into something like proper seamen. Just as the centurions made the Roman legions what they were, and ferocious drill sergeants built the Brigade of Guards, so it was petty officers who really made the Royal Navy. Who could ever forget Charlie Sweet, who taught us PT? "If I can do it," he would say, hurling his incredibly muscular frame into some impossible contortion, "you can do it." Who does not bear scar tissue inflicted by the tongue and eye of the redoubtable gunner's mates, the fearsome "One-Way" Street, the man-eating "Dickie" Bird? With their obsessive spit-and-polish, their fetish for doing everything by numbers, they were of the classic mould of the RN cruiser gunner's mate who, detailed to parade the ship's company before the medical officer for what was euphemistically called "shortarm inspection", concocted the famous drill for the occasion.

All hands were to be fallen in, he told them beforehand, in rig of the day, "with open vents". When the medical officer appeared they would be brought to attention and begin the drill, to a two-part cadence. "On the order 'One!' " he bellowed, "place the right hand smartly on the crotch. Then— wait for it!—on the order 'Two!' out cocks, and I wants to 'ear them foreskins come back with a click!"

From *Naden*, we proceeded up the British Columbia coast to Comox, where we lived under canvas on a sandspit and built a rifle range in sweltering heat while hundreds of burly ratings lay about in the shade, picking their teeth. This was the notion of our commanding officer, an incredible ex-RN lieutenant (retired) who, because of his enormous boots at the end of a long, skinny frame, was known to all simply as "Feets". It was Feets' fixation that officers should command entirely by example, not by orders, and he ran his lot of young toughs like a Girl Guide camp leader. He would attempt to get a boatful of midnight libertymen, returning from the beer parlours of Comox, to sing improving songs, even hymns. Nothing so coarse as "Roll Out the Barrel", of course, or "I've Got Sixpence"; no, he would start off on "Keep the Home Fires Burning", in a quavering falsetto, and insist that we, as officers, pitch in "to show the chaps how". To lift our own shaky tenor into the damp night air before a boatload of snickering sailors while Feets led us in what he believed to be "Onward Christian Soldiers" was an ordeal that left scars we bear to this day.

But we exacted our revenge upon Feets. The culmination of our musketry course was a field exercise; we were divided into two forces, one invading, the other defending, and turned loose to creep about the scrub and do one another in with tins of pebbles, which we rattled when we had a target in sight, to simulate light automatic fire. A third group was told off as umpires, and rendered verdicts, "Dead" or "Alive", on any close or questionable calls.

In practice, of course, once turned loose in the woods we all found a shady spot and settled down, as comfortably as we could, until somebody should blow the whistle and call "Time!" A group of our more desperate spirits who had settled down in a thicket with a deck of cards, peered out on hearing thrashing sounds and spied Feets himself, his ungainly frame bent nearly double, creeping through the underbrush seeking whom he might destroy. The card-players could scarcely believe their good fortune; waiting till Feets was right abreast of them, they let him have it right in the sweetbreads with a furious rattle of their tin of pebbles.

Feets gave it the big effort. Drawing himself to his considerable height, he placed a fluttering hand over his heart, then toppled headlong into a weed patch, as dramatic and moving an exit as any battlefield has ever witnessed.

"Dead," pronounced the umpire, and rejoined the card-players.

Prince Rupert, or simply "Rupert", as everyone called it, was our next port of call. We were based there in a patrol boat, formerly a twin-screw motor yacht, alternating patrols about the virgin wilderness of the Queen Charlotte Islands with long spells swinging around a buoy off Barrett Rock or Metlakatla Pass as examination vessel. When you could see the mountain tops, you knew it would rain shortly; when you couldn't see the mountain tops, it was raining.

The presiding genius of Rupert, and a most appropriate symbol, was a huge and very old totem pole which stood atop the highest hill looking out over the town. It was an incredible thing, signifying heaven-knows-what crisis in the life of the Haida Indians who had put it up there more than a century before. On the top stood a feathered chieftain, grasping his private parts in one hand and brandishing a tomahawk aloft in the other. Obviously, he was about to perform a rather drastic bit of surgery upon himself. Local legend had it than when a virgin should touch the pole, the chief's axe would fall. For years, every girl above the age of ten had touched the pole, but still the axe had not fallen . . .

Rupert in the war years still had much of the aspect of the gold-rush boom days; at night its streets were crowded with fishermen and lumbermen, together with sailors from the Fishermen's Reserve, gunners from the coast artillery battery, and soldiers from the Rocky Mountain Rangers, as hard-bit-ten a regiment as one could find this side of the Foreign Legion. In Rupert's rain-soaked isolation, drinking was the primary recreation, followed, not necessarily in that order, by fighting and fornication. The red-light section on the outskirts of town was known as "Over the Hump", and the girls there took time off every Wednesday afternoon to attend the weekly matinée at the movie theatre downtown; they would arrive in a body, amid cheery greetings, whistles, and feet-stamping from other spectators, and occupy a central section of seats set aside for them.

Rupert was a base of the Fishermen's Reserve, a body of fishermen enrolled by the navy, together with their boats, for patrol duties. They wore naval uniform and painted their ships grey, but otherwise bore their naval responsibilities lightly. The rum, intended to be mixed with water and issued daily as grog, and supplied to the ship in large kegs, was used instead as a sort of communal replenishment for the individ-ual bottles which every man took with him for a run ashore; it was common for a Fishermen's Reserve vessel to go through its quarterly quota in a single night on the town.

Early in our stay at Rupert, a Fishermen's Reserve vessel arrived one evening, and instantly disgorged its entire crew uptown; by the time the last line was secured the only one left aboard as duty watch was a raffish tomcat, and he only because he'd been locked in the gallery. Next morning, the scene on the jetty was like something out of Kipling's "Danny Deever"; the ships' companies of every naval vessel in port were drawn up in hollow square while the base commander himself, resplendent in gold lace, slowly paced along the ranks in the wake of a heavily made-up young lady, a waitress from the Boston café. Someone in naval uniform, she claimed, had pulled her into one of the café's curtained booths and had his way with her; not, one should have thought who was familiar with that café's waitresses, such a difficult thing to do. Still, she had lodged a complaint and the commander himself, anxious for his service's public image, had come down to bring retribution, harsh but just, swiftly home to the miscreant. The little party paced along the pallid ranks, the girl, powdered and petulant, searching every face, the commander glowering in the rear.

By the time they reached the fishermen reservists, everyone present knew that they were close to the mother lode; surely somewhere among all those black eyes, those split lips, those bent noses, was her assailant. Surprisingly, the girl sailed right on past the worse of the walking wounded; the Rocky Mountain Rangers had been in town too, last night, and there'd been the usual friendly punch-up. But she found her man at the end of the line, and stood pointing, with an accusing finger, at the ship's captain himself! With a sheepish smile, the skipper was led away to his fate amid the admiring whistles, hoots, and catcalls of his crew.

It was on the West Coast that we were introduced to the bottomless fund of local knowledge drawn on by veteran coastal sailors. For years, ships of the Canadian National and Canadian Pacific, and of the old Union and Blackball lines, had gone charging through narrow, rock-strewn passages at twenty knots or better, even in thick fog. They did it by precise timing, carefully clocking passage time in good weather at every state of the tide in order to run the same route safely in bad visibility, and by a variety of practices based on the most detailed local knowledge.

We had seen for ourselves how ships traversed steep-sided narrow passages in fog by whistle echoes. The ship blew its whistle frequently, and steered towards the side from which the last echo was received. When the echo came back simultaneously from each side, the ship was in mid-channel; nothing could be simpler.

But the extent of local knowledge possessed by coastal pilots is best illustrated by the story of a steamship official taking passage on one of his own ships, and standing nervously beside his captain, who was taking the ship along at tremendous speed on a thick, foggy night.

Aware that soon a right-angled turn would have to be made, and anxious about the complete lack of any visible shoreline, the worried passenger asked the captain how he would recognize the turning point when it was reached.

"Ah, there's nothing to it," the captain reassured him. "Billy Harrison runs a grocery right on the point, and keeps a dog. I blow the whistle when we get close, and it makes the dog bark. When I hear Billy's dog. I know its time to alter course."

The shore official was appalled to learn that the ship's safety was dependent upon so seemingly slender a thread, but could only hope that the captain was right and that he would hear the dog in time. He joined the captain in the bridge wing, and strained his ear to catch any response as the ship began to sound its whistle.

Nothing. The whistle blew again; still no bark. A third

time—and there, far off, he could distinctly hear the barking of a dog! Excitedly, he turned with a smile to congratulate the captain, but his face fell when he noticed the captain still listening, a hand cupped to his ear.

"But captain! Captain! It's time to alter course! I heard the dog barking just now!"

"No! No! No!" the captain responded impatiently. "That's not Billy's dog!"

Hundreds upon hundreds of Canadian seamen enjoyed the experience, as we did, of bringing a newly built ship from the West Coast around to the Atlantic. Their ports of call—San Diego or San Pedro, or perhaps one of the Mexican ports—may have varied a bit, but one place they are sure to remember is Panama, on the western side of the isthmus pierced by the famous canal. Actually, there are two Panamas, and it was the older, ruined city, rather than the modern one, which fascinated us. For this was the city founded by the Conquistadores, those impossibly romantic figures with associations going back to Drake and Hawkins and the age of pirates. But it was Morgan, the most successful pirate of them all, who finally ended the reign of the old city; it never recovered from his devastating sack, and its great stone ruins lie, overgrown with jungle, all about the native shack-town that lingers on the site.

To someone like me, brought up on pirate stories in countless *Chums* and *Boy's Own Paper* serials, Panama was the most romantic place I had ever seen, and its great gold cathedral altar, once painted white to escape the attentions of Morgan's pirates, and representing the lives of who knows how many Indian slaves and Spanish soldiers, seemed the stuff of pure fantasy. But Panama is also famous for its Cocoanut Grove, a notorious red-light section lined with tiny wooden "cribs", where half-naked little Indian girls displayed their coppery charms and cried out for custom to the passing throngs. VD is endemic among the natives; indeed, it was from the Spanish Main that Columbus's sailors were supposed to have brought syphilis home to Europe for the first time. As officer of the day, it was my job to caution our libertymen about the dangers that lay in wait for the careless or unwary ashore. It seems curious, in retrospect, that a set of grown men, which included grizzled old salts from the China Coast and the River Plate meat trade, steeped in the curious vices of Yokahama and the Reeperbahn, should have accepted the prudish vapourings of a beardless youth with only the sketchiest notions of feminine plumbing, and whose encounters with the opposite sex were limited to a few crowded moments in a parked car. But the bonds of naval discipline are all-pervasive; my strictures were accepted with no more than the usual amount of eye-rolling and smirking. As my libertymen shuffled sheepishly ashore, I doled out condoms with all the sang-froid I could muster; after all, as seagoing sailors, weren't we all men of the world?

For the passage through the Canal, we were boarded by an armed guard, a swaggering fellow with a great service revolver carried assertively on his hip. As a non-belligerent, he said belligerently, the United States was taking no chance with the passage of armed men-of-war through the Canal; he was aboard to ensure there was no monkey business. We gave him a hard time, poor fellow. It was bad enough that we had to fight a chicken-hearted America's war for her without armed guards being sent aboard to terrorize honest sailormen, we told him, and plied him with rum and food. He fell asleep after lunch in the wardroom, when Harvey, the junior sublieutenant, and I, representing the baser element in the mess, stole his revolver and substituted a large, overripe banana in its holster. Such a dither when he awoke to find his beloved pistol gone! We took pity on him at last, of course—it would cost him his job, he assured us—and restored the weapon to him in time for him to hasten ashore in Colon, a thoroughly chastened man.

Kingston, Jamaica, was our next port of call. Italy had just come into the war, and we were based there for a time as one of a force patrolling the Caribbean to intercept Italian ships trying to make a run for home from the U.S. Gulf ports. With all its buccaneering connections, it was a most romantic place, particularly the naval dockyard at the harbour entrance to Port Royal. Now in ruins, it was once home for a host of famous British admirals. Lord Howe had been there, of course, and so had Rodney and Hood and Cornwallis, Saumarez and St. Vincent and the great Nelson himself. A tablet in the wall of Fort Charles, an old battery defending the harbour mouth, reminded us that we were walking in Nelson's footsteps, and urged us to honour his name and remember his fame. With its old signal tower, its sagging roofs and crumbling buildings, the deserted dockyard was a place of infinite romance, enormously appealing to us.

Indeed, we enjoyed our stay in Jamaica; the Myrtle Bank, biggest and best hotel in the island, had been taken over by a branch of the Admiralty and was full of paymasters and nice British Wrens, while a Canadian regiment, the Winnipeg Grenadiers, was on garrison duty there. The regiment was later to be sent to Hong Kong, to be decimated in the horrors of Japanese prison labour camps, but they were lively company for us in Kingston and we saw a good deal of them in the wardroom, particularly the resoundingly named Captain Hook. At Kingston we made the acquaintance of bum-boat women, twentieth-century versions of Little Buttercup, who came aboard to hustle our laundry and set up little stalls alongside to flog souvenirs to gullible matelots. They also dished out cards advertising a wide variety of services ashore—tailors, cleaners, and the like—including such coyly worded invitations as that for "Daisie's Drinking Parlour—drinks, dancing, and you guess the rest!"

But what fascinated us were the cards listing barber services: "Hair dresser to royalty", and then would follow an impressive list of royal notables, from the turn of the century to the present. It turned out that these were princes who had been barbered while serving as naval officers in visiting men-o'-war. We hastened ashore to the establishment with the most resounding list of royal personages on its card, and had our hair cut in a funny little shop looked down upon by a whole gallery of faded photographs of Edwardian admirals and young sprigs of royalty, all bearded like the Pard and all, we thought, viewing the proceedings with a decidedly fishy eye.

Jamaica was beautiful, but the natives were something else; they struck us as surly and morose, with none of that cheerful bounce and light-heartedness that seems so characteristic of the people in the smaller Caribbean islands. A lot of them seemed perpetually dazed with drink or drugs, and there were too many glazed eyes and sullen mutterings for comfort.

Bermuda, our next stop, was a pleasant contrast: small and civilized after all the vivid colour and latent violence of the tropics, and with surely the most pleasant and prosperous native community. We berthed here at Ireland Island, a vast dockyard complex which had been the base of the Royal Navy's West Atlantic Squadron—the one with the rumbustious song, famous in naval messes the world over—during all the long peacetime years of the British Empire. Now used only to service birds of passage, like ourselves, it was a fine example of that amazing chain of superb naval bases spread all around the world by the Royal Navy for its coal-burning fleet, each link within handy steaming distance of the next.

Lying in an enclosed dock while we were there, we could not use the ship's heads and relied instead on toilet facilities built on the shore alongside, and designed to accommodate the ships' companies of a whole squadron of large capital ships. A veritable pantheon of plumbing, it stretched in a long row as far as the eye could see; an endless line of toilet cubicles, all neatly segregated and labelled into a rigid hierarchy.

Such variety of choice. We strolled past dozens of doors, all properly labelled; not for us the seamen's or signalmen's or stokers' facilities, nor those set aside for chief and petty officers. The label "Gunroom officers"—as lowly one-stripers, we were technically such—made us hesitate, but why should we share facilities with scruffy RN snotties and subbies? Next door were premises for lieutenants, but from observation we knew they were not up to much. "Commanders", now—that had a nice ring, and you were likely to meet a nicer class of people there, but it was next door to the facilities set aside for commanding officers, and we did not wish to poach on the privacy of our own skipper. Further on—ah, there was our proper niche! "Flag officers"—it had a nice ring to it; if you're going to go, go first class. It became a point of honour for us henceforth to use the facilities set aside for flag officers; just sitting there, on the seat used before us by all the admirals, was to savour the greatness of our imperial past. We sat, like as not, on the very seat used by Cunningham and Pound, by Beatty and Jellicoe, Fisher and Lord Charles Beresford. Why, surely King George V himself must have been there before us? It was fascinating to conjecture, so that a visit to the shore heads quite made our day.

The presiding genius of the base was Trammy Lee, a lean, elderly Royal Navy lieutenant-commander who seemed to run the whole base himself. Certainly nobody else seemed to be about except this gangling figure, who used to appear, pedalling his bicycle down the deserted quay, with a small terrier carried in the metal basket on the handlebars. Trammy—his nickname, famous throughout the fleet, was due to the circumstance of his having been born on a tram—was one of the RN's eccentrics and something of an old woman, but it was surprising what he could get done in the way of stores or repairs when he got down to it. He was a little severe to us on arrival, having just had an unhappy experience with a

Canadian armed merchant cruiser whose crew had proved a bit fretful, but we got him down in the wardroom and he mellowed a bit. He was full of an impending move to Jamaica; he wasn't at all sure that Susan would settle in there, he told us. He wanted to move, but Susan was dead against it; they had until the weekend to make up their minds. We muttered something sympathetic about wilful wives, only to learn that Susan, on whose decision everything seemed to hinge, was not his wife but his dog, the little terrier who went everywhere with him.

Bermuda was lovelier then than it became in the postwar years; apart from a few service vehicles, there were no cars on the island, and the blight had not yet carried off all the beautiful cedars. A little narrow-guage railway ran from St. George's at one end of the island to Hamilton at the other; the ride, along the very edge of the coast, was a delight in the little open-air coaches. The Canadian navy took over part of the base later in the war as a base for winter work-ups of newly commissioned ships. Most of us, at one time or another, were to experience the high winds and driving rain that are a feature of a Bermuda winter, while huddled at an exposed anchorage in the tiny harbour of St. George's or outside in Five Fathom Hole. Bermuda is a terrible place to approach, with fearful coral reefs far off the land, and only a narrow, buoyed channel winding through the coral around to the capital, Hamilton. One fellow we knew, making the journey around in his new corvette, had been desperately searching for the next buoy marking a turn through a torrential downpour. Spotting the marker in the driving rain, he altered course around it and put himself high and dry on the coral; the "marker" had been a floating crate.

Ireland Island was abandoned when we saw it after the war; grass was growing through the cracked pavements, and roofs were beginning to sag. Its great days as a naval base were a dream, its admirals so many ghosts in the echoing buildings. But surely, if it was haunted, it would be by the shade of a spectral bicycle, bearing an elderly rider and his elderly dog along the lonely jetties and basins over which they watched for so long.

New York, farther north, was a base we were to come to know well. Most Canadian ships and seamen were put on the triangle run, at some stage in life, for their sins. You were based at Halifax, sailed out to Western Ocean Meeting Point south of Newfoundland with an eastbound convoy, traded that for a westward convoy bound for Boston and New York, then trundled back with a third convoy bound for Halifax, home, and beauty. You got the worst of the weather—it got colder and the seas grew steeper as you neared the continental shelf—and all the trouble of meeting and forming up three convoys instead of one on each trip, but the one redeeming feature of the hated triangle run was that you had a good chance of a few days in New York. Gene Kelly and Frank Sinatra sang it for all of us: "New York, New York, it's a wonderful town!" Well, in the war years, at any rate.

If you needed repairs, you went upriver to the Brooklyn Navy Yard, but for most of us the escort berths were all in Staten Island, across the harbour from the big city. It took a long time, but the ferry ride across was lots of fun; after all, that spectacular skyline is something to see, and the harbour traffic, with its big liners and battleships, was always exciting. The long, long rides on the shabby subway weren't much fun, and they meant that any run ashore was going to take some time, but we got accustomed to a night on the town, a long run back to the ship, shave and shower and breakfast, and so ready for the new day. Being young helped.

Of course, we did all the mandatory tourist sights, Radio City, and so on, as well as the big tourist traps like the Latin Quarter. But with experience we managed to carve out some particular niche for ourselves; each group had some particular nightspot where each run ashore wound up. A marvellous officers' club operated at Delmonico's, with food and drink and music and the most dazzling girls imaginable; a great place to get acquainted. For some reason or other, our escort group adopted Jimmy Kelly's as its rendezvous, a little bistro in Greenwich Village that vibrated to a solid beat that virtually eliminated conversation. With other ships, it was other places; the *Mina*'s wardroom, for example, headed in a body for the Hotel Pierre, where Xavier Cugat, the Cuban king of the rumba, held sway. Cugat was an accomplished cartoonist as well as a bandleader, and he ran off marvellous crayon caricatures of his *Minas* fans; in return, their wardroom in harbour resounded to "one, two, three, kick!" records night and day, and any visitor on entering was likely to be tossed a bongo or a pair of maracas by Johnny Kingsmill and expected to pitch in. New York was everyone's favourite port of call, although a bad place to be in its frequent fog. I remember heaving to off the Ambrose light-vessel, waiting for some unseen ship to get clear of the channel. Nearer and nearer she came, her deep-toned siren so loud and close that it seemed to shake the very air. Suddenly, only feet away, a tremendous cliff towered over us, so high that it cut off the sun filtering through the fog. For a heart-stopping moment the *Queen Mary* hung above us, so close that we could see every scuttle, every rivet-head, filling the world with the roaring sound of her passage through the water. Her siren boomed out, high above, and then she was past us, bellowing out to sea like some maddened bull elephant. If you ran into anything off New York, it was likely to be something pretty solid.

To most corvette types, St. John's, Newfoundland, was home. Western base of the mid-ocean groups, frequent port of call for escorts on the triangle run, and supply base for the support groups of frigates and destroyers, its jetties were jammed with the fighting craft of every Allied nation, and the harbour centre was cluttered with merchantmen in for emergency repairs. For months, a ship was berthed at the trot-buoys with a torpedo hole blasted clean through her at the water-line, a hole so vast and cavernous that motorboats crossing the harbour used to take a short cut right through her. Even now, after the passage of so many years, one has only to close one's eyes to see—and smell—and hear—it all again: the reek of cod, the shrieking gulls, the rows of salt-stained hulls, three and four deep, along the South Side wharves; the misty sun, warm on the pale greens and pinks and whites of Western Approaches camouflage, the shades of grey of ships from other commands. Escorts berthed on the south side of the harbour, at the foot of the bare hills which fruit-starved sailors used to comb for blueberries in season. Astern of us the big Portuguese sailing ships, crammed with cod from the Banks, would lie before making the long passage home, their decks crowded with friendly brown-faced seamen from the Algarve. Merchantmen berthed at the quays along the north side, or in the city itself, or underwent repairs at the yard at the top of the harbour. Huddled in out-of-the way corners were the antique steamers of the sealing fleet, pencil-thin funnels rising from clipper-bowed wooden hulls. Lying derelict at a dilapidated wharf was the hulk of the *Calliope*, once a famous sloop-of-war in the Victorian Royal Navy and later a drill-ship, now housed over and used as a salt-storage hulk, with an old Hotchkiss gun drooping forlornly from a casemate. It was a busy, animated scene, full of the sights and

sounds and smells of the wartime North Atlantic, and a fascinating place to be.

We were a polyglot bunch at the escort berths; British and
Canadian ships mingled with Polish and Norwegian destroyers, Free French corvettes. The Poles were fire-eaters, and
their ships, named for thunder and lightning and the like, reflected this flair. They also enjoyed a reputation as tremendous womanizers; the standard joke was of a Polish officer
who, after exchanging names with a girl he'd just met, ex-
claimed: "Enoff of thees loff-making; let's fock!"

The Free French were something else; their ships stank
like a stable, and they thought nothing of urinating on the
deck. We would watch, fascinated, as sweaty French seamen
would struggle out of dirty clothes, douse themselves in
fragrant lotion, then pull clean jumpers over their unwashed
torsos and go ashore looking like a million dollars. With their
striped jumpers and red pompoms, their uniforms had a flair
and flamboyance all their own. But their emphasis was on
panache rather than cleanliness; even on a lowly corvette,
they saluted their ensign at "Sunset" and morning "Colours"
with a bugler. Although the bugle itself was green and battered, and the bugler grubby in shabby gaiters and stained
uniform, it completely outclassed our measly bosun's pipe.
And they got the job done; their corvette *Aconit* bagged two
U-boats in a single crossing.

The cream of the crop were the Norwegians; they had so
many top officers and experienced men for so few ships—a
handful of old British destroyers loaned them by the RN—
that they were reputed to use full commanders as watch-
keepers. It was a treat to watch them come alongside, with
hardly a word spoken; everyone knew his job and did it
quickly and quietly.

In the later afternoon, when the day's work was done, we
used to poke along the jetties seeing what ships had arrived,
and visit with old friends. In couples or in groups, off we'd
trudge for the long walk around the head of the harbour to
the city, and the fleshpots of Newfyjohn. These were few in
number and austere in amenities, but nonetheless they were
savoured to the full. One could—and did—send a telegram
from the cable office to one's girl back home in Canada or go
shopping in Bowring's or one of the other delightfully Victorian emporiums along Water Street; where else could you select a pair of Eskimo-made sealskin boots out of an
odoriferous barrel?

A favourite café along Water Street advertised "The best milkshakes east of Boston"; since they were also the *only* milkshakes east of Boston, the claim was a valid one. As a concession to the curious tastes of Canadian and American customers, hot dogs were also prepared at a steamy glass partition behind the marble-topped counter, but upstairs in the dining-room everything was starched British gentility. Groups of sailors from Poland, Norway, and Senegal mingled with cropped Canadian youngsters at the little tables, behaving with the decorum expected in such surroundings; flowered wallpaper and potted palms provided the decor and elderly waitresses in starched uniforms served the tables. From time to time a little phonograph in the corner was re-wound and another Strauss waltz was played as a discreet background for polite conversation.

It was all like some vanished English tea-room, glimpsed in a fading sepia print in a Victorian snapshot album, and we loved it. Nothing could have been in greater contrast to the rough masculine world of the messdecks than this primly spinsterish place, and fellows from the ships packed it, night after night. After that, one could climb the steep hills to either of the two movie theatres; Jimmy Cagney was very big at "The Popular Star", as one of the houses modestly called itself. There were lots of big and bouncy and popular dances for enlisted men at the Caribou Hut, or at the fine modern hostel run by the K. of C. people. The terrible fire which destroyed it, and snuffed out so many young lives, was one of the war's real tragedies. For the escape arrangements had broken down, and youngsters died in queues at the very exits.

Choice was more limited for officers; mostly we picked our way down to Water Street to make the great climb up the famous fifty-nine steps of the spindly outside staircase that led to The Crowsnest, in a loft high above the old Outerbridge warehouse.

If any single place could be said to be the heart of the corvette navy, the Crowsnest, officially entitled the Seagoing Officers Club, would be it. Certainly it was home to all of us in the escort ships; a place you could drop into at any time of day or night and be assured of a welcome, a drink, or a simple snack—the hot ersatz eggs and Spam sandwiches were always good—from the assiduous Gordon and his wife, who presided there. Dozens of enormous leather armchairs were scattered about the bare floor, and grouped about the fireplace, with its comfortable padded fender. The walls were resplendent with the crest of every escort ship in the western ocean; original works of art, most of them, and always worth a tour of inspection to see what new ones had been added since the last visit. In a corner, the head of a large spike, "Spikenard's Spike", protruded from the floor; it had been driven in there by Shadforth, commanding officer of the corvette *Spikenard*, during a nail-hammering contest on his last night ashore before *Spikenard* sailed. She was torpedoed and lost with all hands, and her spike in the Crowsnest floor was retained as a memento of absent friends.

Although Newfyjohn was a naval base of world significance, it wore a curiously impermanent air, like a travelling tent show. Unlike the vast and inconsequential base built by the Americans in the wilderness of nearby Argentia, there were no naval shore facilities at St. John's. Mainguy and his staff operated out of the Newfoundland Hotel, the ships berthed at the rickety South Side wharves, and training and repair facilities were housed in a depot ship provided by the Royal Navy. HMS *Forth*, a magnificent modern depot ship with every sort of machine shop and repair facility as well as crew training and amenity space, was our first ship's home on the South Side, and she was replaced by HMS *Greenwich*, an older, smaller vessel. Unlike the army and air force, both with big permanent installations, the navy at St. John's seemed to operate out of its hat; when it closed up shop at the war's end it left nothing to mark its passing but a tradition and a few genes in the Newfoundland bloodstrain. But for all of that, Newfyjohn lives on in the memory of thousands of corvette sailors as a warm and outgoing place, the home of hospitable and friendly people and of the finest, most efficient escort base in all the North Atlantic.

Its counterpart at the other end of the mid-ocean "milk run" was Londonderry, in Northern Ireland. To arrive at Derry after a hard east-bound crossing was a little like approaching the pearly gates. After rounding Inishtrahull, you picked up the green and pleasant coast. The sea calmed as you approached the estuary, and off-watch officers and men shaved and changed into smart shoregoing uniforms. Carpets and linen cloths reappeared in the wardroom, open scuttles admitted air and sunlight to stuffy messdecks. An air of cheery expectancy filled the ship, and it was wonderful to feel the luxury of clean, soft shirts after living for weeks in clothes stiff with salt. And then you entered the mouth of the river Foyle, and the wonderful green land enfolded you.

God! How green Ireland was; the Emerald Isle, for sure! After weeks of flat, grey horizons, grey seas, grey skies, how marvellous to be wrapped about with green hills, trees, fields! Even the old ruined castle tower on the nearby shore was draped in ivy and called—what else?—Greencastle. The sounds of the shore were indescribably sweet: the ecstasy of soft birdsong, after shrieking seabirds!

The Foyle must surely be one of the loveliest of rivers, an escape from the sea unmarred by industrial ugliness. In the escort groups, we filed upriver in a state of bliss, enraptured by the beauty of fields and flowers and trees growing right to the water's edge; truly, Mother Earth had clasped us to her warm bosom after all the perils and privations of the sea! We fuelled at a tanker off Moville, a little estuary village, then picked up a pilot from his tiny skiff for the trip up the narrow, winding river to Derry itself, a beautiful old city in a lovely valley setting. On the outskirts, in a stretch of walled gardens running down to the water, we would come in sight of a fine old country house lying in extensive grounds. Instantly, from an upper window would come the bright officious winking of an Aldis signal light, for this was Boom, or Broome—nobody seemed sure of its correct spelling—Hall, home of the Wrens who staffed the base so efficiently, and who also included some of the finest and fastest signallers in the business. The winking light would send along time and place of that night's dance—there was always a dance in Derry—and our signalman would respond with the number of fellows we would be landing to attend, and another fine party would be in the making. If we were arriving after office hours, the lawns would be alive with uniformed girls waving and calling out to the passing ships. It was the final touch needed to bring us back to the wonderful world of the shore; by the time we rounded the final bend and came in sight of the escorts crowded at their berths along the western bank, all our weariness, all the fatigue of the long trip behind us was forgotten. Home is the sailor, home from the sea. . . .

Everyone loved Derry; the shops of Shipquay street, the battered beauty of the old cathedral, the cheerful chatter of the Shakespearean Cellar bar, the soft laughter, lilting voices, and fresh complexions of its Irish girls! Nice, old-fashioned girls, too, who took a dim view of any "larking about", but were always ready for a dance or "the pictures" or a Sunday picnic in the soft green loveliness of the Irish countryside.

Stop-overs in Derry were all too short, and busy with

painting and storing and training, yet they had an idyllic
quality that captured the imagination of the most prosaic. It
is said that when the last of the escort groups sailed down-
river from the empty base at war's end, every Wren lined the
lawns of Boom Hall, waving—and weeping—as the ships
filed by. And the men waving from the ships—they wept, too.

Earlier in the war, we had been based at Greenock, a
suburb of Glasgow which, with its streetcars and cheery
bustle, seemed a sort of Scottish Toronto. Later, at Iceland,
we were based at Hvalfjord, around the corner from
Reykjavik, or Rinkeydink as everyone called it, and a more
dreadful anchorage it would be hard to find. There were no
shore facilities and everyone tried to anchor off in a fjord so
deep that good holding ground was impossible to find. Midwinter gales would be funnelled down the anchorage from
the mountains all about us, shrieking blizzards that blotted
out everything and sent ships dragging down into each other
or into the minefields. The destroyer *Skeena* was blown onto
the reefs in a midnight gale and was lost with fifteen men,
drowned in blinding snow and sea. This nighmarish place had
an appropriately eery sentinel; far out at sea a great tooth of
jagged rock stood out of the grey waves, its towering top
swirling with seabirds, their plaintive cries somehow em-
phasizing the desolate loneliness of this tiny pillar of land in
the vast desert of the ocean.

Iceland was a ghastly place, particularly in midwinter, and
the people there, even the frosty blondes at the Hotel Borg's
dinner dance, were as cold and inhospitable as their barren
land. Our only touch of warmth was to be found in the
wardrooms of *Hecla* and *Vulcan*, the American and British
depot ships, respectively, where good food and good company
brought a ray of civilized comfort into this bleak and savage
place. We made a lot of friends, too, among the American
destroyers stationed there in their pre-war "neutrality patrol"
days: the *Reuben James* and the *Kearney*, both later torpedoed; the *Simpson* and the *McCormack* and the *Broom*.
They seemed to us, with their peacetime complements and
primitive instrumentation and weaponry, like something out
of the Stone Age; who will forget the shock of seeing their
funny little "y" guns, as they called their depth-charge
throwers, used as a rack for securing mops and deck gear?
The truth is, the Americans never did catch up in anti-submarine warfare; after the bloodbath off their Atlantic coasts fol-

lowing their entry into the war, all Atlantic convoying was taken over by British and Canadian escorts, with a few U.S. coastguard cutters thrown in, because the United States needed its ships in the Pacific. The Pacific belonged to them, we felt; the Atlantic to us.

Apart from the principal bases, most Canadian seamen had some particular favourite port of call. For some it was Horta or Ponta Delgada in the Azores, those mid-ocean mountain tops where escorts would sometimes visit briefly to refuel. Being Portuguese, they were neutral, and a little gunboat would puff out fussily to check out the most powerful man-o'-war arriving off the breakwater. The contrast between these semi-tropical paradises, with their flowers and fruit and music, with the wintry wastes of the North Atlantic we'd left behind was unbelievable. To leave a hard-pressed convoy one night and be dining ashore on an open-air terrace the next, amid good food and wine and with the moon rising behind the awesome peak of Pico, was like a kind of magic, as was the Merry Widow setting of sidewalk cafés, mosaic pavements, and gold-laced officers in tasselled knee-boots from the turreted fort, sipping hot chocolate in tall glasses.

For some seamen, Quebec was the favourite port of call. We were based there briefly, escorting troopships to the new air bases being built at Goose Bay in Labrador and Thule in Greenland. Quebec City, with its pretty girls and gaiety, its Grande Allée and Dufferin Terrace, its parties at the baronial Château and picnics at Montmorency Falls, was a delightful place, and the war seemed far away. About the only "military" we saw were the "Quebec Highlanders" as the local girls wryly referred to the loose-gowned monks from the city's numerous religious orders. Yet it was out of this bright and beautiful city and its placid St. Charles basin that we lost a lot of ships, and one fateful night on the Labrador coast, our "chummy ship", the corvette *Shawinigan*, vanished in a moment, torpedoed and lost with all hands; so many friendly, familiar faces we would never see again.

My own particular favourite was the old naval base of Devonport at Plymouth in England. It was a wonderful place to come into from the sea, turning sharp left at the Eddystone and sailing into the beautiful Sound, surely one of the world's loveliest harbours. We always felt the drama of the war at sea when entering or leaving that harbour, steaming past the great natural grandstand of the Hoe and its terraces, thick with crowds of strollers. With the ship in good trim and crew fallen in, fore and aft, in smart rig of the day, we felt ourselves the cynosure of all eyes in a real showcase of a place after the drab anonymity of most naval ports. Then up into the Hamoaze, an estuary heavy with history, and the dockyard, cradle of half the British fleet, with its great basins and drydocks filled with vast battle-wagons bearing famous names and in various states of disrepair, like duchesses caught with their hair down and their corsets off. In a grubby little office ashore at Flagstaff Steps, an elderly Captain D, with an even more venerable Wren as apparently his sole assistant, ran a good part of the Channel war, sending flying squads of cruisers and heavy-gunned destroyers off on raids against enemy shipping, and escort groups of fearsome power and prowess off to make life miserable for any U-boats rash enough to enter his part of the Channel. The contrast with our own base staffs, where every assistant had several assistants and it took an act of God to authorize movement of a garbage scow across the harbour, was a refreshing one to us, as was Captain D's brisk and informal greeting when you called at his office for orders: "Morning, *Camrose*; little job of work for you today!" He'd then send you halfway round Europe on the most complex operation.

Lying at Devonport, you were in the heart of a great naval base, with a big city fire-bombed into a kind of garden centre, behind it. Yet you could drift off in the ship's whaler in the opposite direction, and sail up the St. Germans river into the most idyllic of English countrysides.

Devon, glorious Devon. For our money, Plymouth was the best base of all.

7
THE OLD FIRM

~~~~~~

We met the Royal Navy's Home Fleet returning to its Iceland lair after hunting *Bismarck* to her doom. Our group were bound in for Hvalfjord after bringing an eastbound convoy across, steaming along in line abreast in the gathering darkness of the late Arctic afternoon.

The fleet caught up with us from astern, their silhouettes popping up above the misty grey of the distant horizon. First there had been the aircraft, carrier-borne planes these, rather than the long-range aircraft we were accustomed to meet so far out at sea. In tight circles they thundered low over the water, searching ahead of the fleet on a broad front, and after them had come the destroyers: big, modern, heavily gunned fellows, not the salty veterans we were familiar with in the Western Approaches. On they came, a dozen or more, zigzagging by a timed pattern, lean and hungry and ferocious, like a pack of hungry hounds. Behind them came the cruisers, the most beautiful of ships, the triple turrets and raked funnels of modern light cruisers mingled with the rather Victorian silhouettes of the bigger County and Town classes. Our bridge quickly overflowed with officers, some with binoculars and others bent over our dog-eared copy of Jane's, identifying these new and glamorous visitors to our realm. Famous names they wore, but look there, astern of them! Here came the big fellows, the great battlewagons with their attendant carrier: the twin-funnelled silhouette of the *King George* v, and the prodigious, triple-turreted mammouth that could only be HMS *Rodney*.

It was an awesome sight as the great fleet swept up our starboard beam and passed us; a blend of speed and power, of science and fighting purpose, the like of which none of us had ever seen before. The fierce destroyers, the magnificent cruisers, all speed and swift striking force, and then the awful menace of the great battleships and the hulking carrier, the very embodiment of brute strength and punishing power.

It was *Rodney* that drew our fascinated gaze: that prodigious fo'c'sle, seemingly half a mile long, dominated by those three immense turrets, mounting nine of the greatest guns ever fitted in a battleship, the enormous sixteen-inchers which had literally shot *Bismarck* to pieces. Behind this endless fo'c'sle, that pyramid of turrets, rose a huge tower of armour plate—and then the ship came to an abrupt end. She was all bows, all bite up forward, with nothing behind it; a great, misshapen, malformed monster waddling past, yet so awesome in her pugnacity that she was utterly magnificent. The great dark shapes swept past us, disappearing in the gathering dusk ahead and leaving us bobbing in their wake. It was dark night when we crept up Hvalfjord into our anchorage; nothing could be seen of the fleet that we knew lay all about us.

But such sights—and sounds—as greeted us next morning. Hvalfjord must be one of the grimmest, bleakest anchorages in all the world, rimmed about with snowy wastes and great ice-peaked mountains. Yet this ghastly place was gay with colour and sound; all about us lay the great capital ships of the Home Fleet, their quarterdecks bright with sauntering officers and pipeclayed marine guards. Marine bands marched and countermarched across the vast teak decks as if on parade, the bright brass and silver of their instruments winking in the pale northern sunshine, the music bright and gay as they played popular light music and brisk Sousa marches. From the corvettes, we stared enthralled at this cloud of butterflies that had settled into our bleak base. Speedy motorlaunches plied from ship to ship, surging alongside spotless teak gangways, or lying at the boat-booms rigged out from each ship's side. It was the magic half-hour before the ceremony of Colours began the working day, and officers promenaded their quarterdecks, taking the air after breakfast, and sailors leaned over the rails, enjoying the last cigarette before turning-to.

From a dozen ships, a dozen bugles, amplified by a hundred loudspeakers, sounded; the ritual of Divisions was about to begin the official service day.

We watched spellbound as the beautiful pageantry unfolded, so familiar from our training days ashore but so much more significant here at sea, in its proper setting. At a word, ten thousand men were suddenly capless, their heads bowed in prayer. At a command, soundless from our distance, the sun flashed on the serried steel of hundreds of bayonets as marine guards presented arms. And then, across the water from each ship, came the slow, measured, mellow music of "The King". From each ship's deck enormous white ensigns, startling in their purity and vivid with the red and blue of their crosses slowly climbed the great stern staffs, each capped with a bright gilt crown. Never had the symbolism of this moment, the reverent act of subservience by all the ship's company to the great standard which embodied nation and sovereign and service, impressed us so deeply; for the first time we could understand the worship which the legions of Imperial Rome had rendered to their legionary standards, enshrined in their own chapels; to men bound in disciplined service, the standards which embodied their corporate dedication were objects of compelling devotion. The moment quickly passed; the ensigns were made fast, the ships' companies dispersed to their myriad duties, and the marine bands marched themselves off parade to a lively quick-step.

We had been privileged to see the two faces of the Royal Navy. The reality of sea-power; the raw, brute force concentrated in a fleet of enormous ships and aircraft, we had seen on a dark winter's afternoon; this force, lying in this remote place, embodied the command of the seas of the western world, controlled the destinies of millions of people unaware of its very existence. The other face was that of the hallowed routines and traditions and pageantry which the Royal Navy carried about with it, bringing order and beauty and civilized standards to the bleakest Arctic anchorage, the hottest sun-baked atoll.

It was easy to lose sight of the purpose behind the charm, to regard, as some silly people did, the navy as effete, a Victorian anachronism in a harsh twentieth-century world of air power and total war. But nobody who served with the Royal Navy had any such illusions; they knew from experience that the RN was not merely tough and competent and professional, but ruthless, too. What other navy would snuff out a potential threat from a former friend, as the British did at Oran when they attacked the French fleet, or send a battleship through all the hazards of a narrow fjord to exterminate a nest of German destroyers, as the Admiralty did with *Warspite* at Nar-

vik? For all its old-world grace and charm, the Royal Navy
would cut the throat of its grandmother if it served its interest, and you'd better believe it!

The truth is, the Royal Navy is not a mere fighting service
at all, in the ordinary sense of the word. It ranks, with the
Catholic Church and the Roman legion, as one of the su-
preme creations of human organizing genius, an institution
which simply defies comparison with its contemporaries. It is
the mother and father of all the world's navies; there is not,
today, a single navy whose organization, uniform, terminol-
ogy, tradition, and technique does not stem from that of the
British Royal Navy.

The Royal Navy is as much a state of mind as a collection
of ships. For all its traditional reticence and modesty, "winning" is what the Silent Service is all about, and all the long
centuries of accumulated triumph have induced in the service
an assumption of ultimate victory particularly galling to rival
navies which know themselves to be superior by every
material standard. The Italian battle fleet was a superb, modern force, for example, vastly superior to the First World
War antiques which were all the British could muster in the
Mediterranean, yet always it was the British who sought, the
Italians who dreaded, an all-out confrontation. There was
never the slightest doubt in British minds—or in Italian!—as
to the ultimate outcome, whatever the apparent disparity in
material strength. The RN had tremendous élan, enormous
confidence and morale, and we found that it rubbed off on
the least of us who flew the white ensign. We were proud of
being Canadian, of course, and painted maple leaves on our
funnels to make sure we got the message across to the
Limeys, but for all of that we were very proud to be a part
of the big show, a Canadian branch of the old Grey Funnel
Line, a member of the White Ensign club, and a sharer of all
that marvellous mystique that went with it.

The Royal Navy's air branch demonstrated another curious
aspect of the Senior Service. To visit the Fleet Air Arm was
to walk back in time to the beginnings of military flight,
when the first scout planes were flown over the trenches of
the First World War by daring young men from the Royal
Naval Flying Corps.

So far as we could see, nothing much had changed in the
Fleet Air Arm since. At the RCAF base in Dartmouth we had
watched, without interest, a succession of sleekly modern aircraft thundering off to go about their various chores, their an-

nonymous crews concealed inside their great cabins. These were air-force machines, but in a lull between their comings and goings we saw a knot of men wheel a little airplane out onto the tarmac. A few minutes later it went whizzing along past us and soared aloft—a tiny single-engined biplane, all canvas and wire and open cockpit. Its two-man crew were gloved and helmeted, its observer in the rear waggling an old-fashioned Lewis gun on a scarfe mounting, and, by God, its pilot even had a long silk scarf trailing back in the slipstream. Up, up, and away! After the Red Baron! We had just been privileged to see the navy's Fairey Swordfish in action, and to anyone brought up, as we had been, on a diet of boys' stories of Spads and Fokkers and Sopwith Camels, she was simply irresistible. Why, it was *Wings!* and *The Dawn Patrol* all over again; like Richard Barthelmess we knew it was madness to send a boy up in a crate like that.

On closer acquaintance, of course, we grew to respect the little Swordfish and her skilled and gutty crews. We watched them land on the rearing decks of tiny Woolworth carriers swept by winter gales, saw them tip the balance of the U-boat war in our favour as they bridged the "Pit" far from land-based air cover. But always we adored them as an anachronism, a reflection of the instinctive RN tendency to cling to the old, the tried-and-true.

But if the Swordfish took one back to the brave days of the First World War, the navy's Walrus transported us back to the very Stone Age of flight, to the primeval beginnings of the powered aircraft. The Walrus had to be seen to be believed, as we found for ourselves when we inspected one aboard HMS *Rodney* in the anchorage at Hvalfjord. It was a stubby, two-winged amphibian not much bigger than a canvas-covered canoe, which it closely resembled, and it was powered, if that is the word, by a tiny engine mounted behind the pilot and his observer, turning a wooden propeller which *pushed* the aircraft, rather than pulled it in the normal manner accepted by God and man. It was sometimes suggested by irreverent sailors that its crew also had to pedal with their feet to keep it aloft, but this does not appear to have been the case.

Yet whatever the Walrus may have lacked in speed and power, it more than made up for in its method of launching, as we found when our host aboard *Rodney,* glancing at his watch, urged us to down our drinks and go on deck to see the fun. We did so and joined the crowd, all in carnival mood, gathered about the old Walrus perched on its catapult amidships. The two Fleet Air Arm officers who formed its crew were checking out final details, assisted by suggestions from the onlookers. (Be sure to wind the elastic, mind.) In their oil-spattered overalls and air of dedicated purpose, they were regarded by their shipmates with affection and not a little awe, appropriate to the practitioners of an art bordering more closely on the occult than on modern science.

Eventually, the plane's crew aboard, catapult trained outboard, and spectators removed to a respectful distance, the engine was started and the wooden blades whirled around to a noise like that of an outboard motor. In his open cockpit, protected only by a tiny windscreen, the ashen-faced pilot gestured with his hand. There was a tremendous explosion, a cloud of acrid smoke, and the Walrus was no longer with us. We had just a glimpse of two goggled heads being snapped backward by the explosion and of the little machine being hurled into space like a sack of potatoes, and then there was simply nothing there.

The Walrus had been projected overside by the force of a gun-cotton explosive charge, only to fall like a stone out of sight. But from somewhere beneath the deck came a sound like an angry wasp; there was a rush for the rail, and from there we could see the Walrus, its engine flat out, skimming bravely over the sea at a pace markedly faster than a man could run. Minutes later it had gained masthead height, and was still climbing manfully upward. It was scheduled to circle the anchorage before landing on the water alongside and we wanted to stay and watch, but our host was wiser, in the ways of the Walrus.

"Come on below and have the other half," he urged us. "It takes the ruddy thing half the day to fly all the way around the anchorage."

His advice proved sound. When we stole a peep outside five minutes later, the Walrus was only just beginning its circuit, and it was not until nearly lunch-time that the little machine landed and taxied across the water to the ship's side. It was quickly hoisted inboard by the ship's crane, and the two intrepid birdmen were gently led below by sympathetic shipmates who pressed restoratives into their hands. The whole thing had been a harrowing adventure, fraught with every sort of peril, and we were conscious of having witnessed an achievement comparable with the first flight of the Wright brothers at Kittyhawk.

There was a whiff of the primeval in everything the Royal Navy did, from flying to flushing a toilet; it was another facet of the legendary Royal Navy mystique.

I remember a glimpse of a man who, perhaps best of all, was the living embodiment of that mystique. He had been knighted and made an admiral by the time we saw him, and ours was surely the smallest ship in his whole command, but for all that it was a great thing to have served under him and we were proud to make the claim. Rear-Admiral Sir Philip Vian was the very image of the dashing naval officer—bold, resourceful, and, above all, successful. More than that, he looked the part—tall, lean, hawk-faced.

It was Vian who had taken *Cossack* into Alten Fjord, laid her alongside the prison ship *Altmark*, and sent a boarding party *armed with cutlasses* to carry off scores of liberated British seamen in the teeth of hostile gunboats and vacillating politicians. It was Vian's destroyers who had hung on to *Bismarck* all through that long, fatal last night, snapping at her heels and delivering her, exhausted and without hope, to her waiting executioners next morning. It was Vian who, with only a handful of light cruisers and destroyers, had held the Italian battle fleet in play and brought his vital convoy through unscathed in the Battle of Sirte: "The most masterly naval action of the war", according to his superiors. It was he who commanded a thousand ships—nine hundred and ninety-nine and *ours!*—in Overlord, the greatest amphibious assault in history, and who went on to command the British carriers in the final operations against the Japanese fleet. Oh, he was a great man, right enough, but what finally established him as a living legend was an incident that happened when he was commissioning a new ship in Scapa Flow, and had assembled the ship's company about him on the quarterdeck for the traditional first-day pep-talk.

As he spoke, a diesel drifter, one of the boats that lugged potatoes and brussel sprouts and other vital supplies out to the anchored ships, went plugging along near by, its one-lung diesel engine growing louder and more obtrusive as it approached.

"Now listen to me, you chaps," said Vian.

Punga! Punga! Punga! went the diesel, louder than ever.

It was too much. Vian stopped, turned dramatically, and bent his fierce glare upon the offending drifter. Incredibly, impossibly, the drifter's engine choked and stopped; it drifted on in sudden silence.

Without any further ado, the great man turned back and resumed his address. Henceforth, his reputation was made; on the lower deck, they knew he could walk on water if he wished to do so; success would attend his every venture.

Yet for all his dash and glamour, Vian, like Cunningham and the rest of the great admirals, had to yield pride of place to a relatively junior officer who had risen from peacetime obscurity to become the one real naval genius of the Second World War. No one man won the Battle of the Atlantic, but certainly no one man did more to win it than Captain Frederick John Walker, Royal Navy. It was one of the war ironies that this great man, the Nelson of his age, should have lived and died virtually unknown outside the service, while lesser men enjoyed public acclaim and world recognition.

Walker was, in every sense of the word, a genius, and all his many and remarkable gifts were concentrated in the special field of hunting and killing U-boats. He had an uncanny gift for anticipating the moves of his underwater antagonists, but it was his original mind, which devised new and devastating anti-submarine techniques, that truely set him apart. It was Walker who was the first, and most enthusiastic, proponent of the support groups: forces of highly trained ships which would act outside the close escort of convoys and, freed of any responsibilities for the safe passage of the convoy, could concentrate on hunting and killing U-boats. It was Walker who refined the depth-charge attack into a fine art, a matter of infinite precision and deliberation, and who developed the famous "creeping attack," in which one ship steamed slowly astern of her submerged prey in constant asdic contact, and directed a consort onto the target, where it subjected the invisible U-boat to a devastating and concentrated rain of depth-charges. It was Walker who developed the notion of an élite group of specially designated ships, the finest available, fitted with the latest devices and crewed by specialists.

Walker built his famous Second Escort Group into the most efficient, the most successful, team of sub-hunters and killers ever seen. His group simply annihilated all the U-boats in its path as it swept across the Atlantic, or lurked "in the deep field" astern of a threatened convoy. On a single trip across, his group sank six submarines, and took the entire crew of one of them prisoner. He became the dread of the U-boat crews; once in contact, he never gave up, turn and twist as the U-boat would. "The Boss", as he was called, would preside inside a ring of escorts established about him, and, the U-boat contacted, he would call out ships one at a time to "have a go". If the ship failed to produce results, he would send her back to the patrolling ring and summon another in her place. A brooding, solitary man, he was given to moments of inspiration, and he had the courage and confidence to act on them.

But above all, it was the precision of his attacks and his resourcefulness under difficulties which set him apart from lesser senior officers. In a celebrated instance, gaining contact with a U-boat late one night after an arduous and tiring day, Walker detailed two ships to maintain contact with the enemy while off-watch officers and men got some much-needed sleep. "We shall attack at 7:30 a.m. and sink her before breakfast," he announced, and the following morning he did just that. The attack began precisely on time, and at ten minutes to eight the group were gathering bits of flotsam from the destroyed U-boat as evidence of another kill, before sending hands to breakfast.

On another occasion, off Iceland, he was faced with a U-boat operating so deep that the group's depth-charges were unable to get below her before detonating. Depth-charges are fired by a hydrostatic pistol; water enters a tiny hole as the charge sinks and detonates it at the desired depth. Walker solved the challenge of the too-deep U-boat in his own way. He put a dab of soft soap in the hole of his depth-charge pistols. The extra sinking time required to wash away the soap was sufficient to take his charges deep enough to destroy the U-boat; "The Boss" had done it again!

I remember late in the war, seeing EG 2, Walker's renowned group, leaving St. John's harbour for sea. Beautiful ships they were: new Bird-class sloops, with lots of free-board to carry the armament and instruments in the wild Atlantic weather.

Starling was Walker's own ship; the others bore names like *Woodpecker, Wren, Wild Goose, Cygnet, Kite*. They were beautiful ships, beautifully maintained, but it was the élan and esprit de corps of the crews that really set EG 2 apart. As the ships turned into the wind, the pennant numbers hoisted at one yard-arm would suddenly vanish and simultaneously be broken out on the other and leeward side, so that the pennants should at all times stream clear of the rigging. Everything was done at the jump; lines and fenders disappeared like magic; as the group filed down harbour, in

tight formation, crews fallen in smartly fore and aft, the
ship's loudspeakers blared a brassy rendition of "A-hunting
we will go". It was a tremendous spectacle, and I was lucky
to see the group at its peak; within days Walker, who virtually lived on his bridge night and day, was dead of exhaus-
tion. But his spirit and techniques were an inspiration to all
of us in the Western Approaches.

He was borne out to sea for the last time in the destroyer
Hesperus, to the shrilling of bosun's pipes, while the crews of
ships in the Gladstone dock lined the rails, with heads bared
and bowed. In the funeral oration earlier in Liverpool Cathedral, Admiral Sir Max Horton, commander-in-chief, Western
Approaches, had delivered his epitaph: "His spirit returns
unto God who gave it. Not dust nor the light weight of stone,
but all the sea of the Western Approaches shall be his tomb."

A different sort of naval occasion was the August 1941 Atlantic Charter meeting of President Roosevelt and Prime
Minister Winston Churchill at Argentia in Placentia Bay. Our
group was taken off its usual mid-ocean milk run, and sent
round instead to Argentia, then just a fog-shrouded dent in
the south coastline of Newfoundland, as escort to the Shell
tanker *Clam.* We soon learned that the *Clam* was to rendezvous with *Prince of Wales,* the big new British battleship,
which would be carrying Winston Churchill together with the
chiefs of staff and the British cabinet to meet with President
Roosevelt and their U.S. opposite numbers. When we arrived
Clam went in and anchored, like a placid cow, off the thickly
forested coast; the rest of us stayed outside and patrolled the
wide, fog-bound entrance.

The Americans were first on the scene: *Augusta,* a cruiser,
with the President aboard; the cruiser *Tuscaloosa;* and the
ancient battle-wagon *Arkansas,* a strange old relic with those
distinctive American basket-work masts. They went in and
anchored while the destroyers of the escort joined us in our
endless quadrille across the harbour mouth, their senior officer, the *McDougall,* nattering away to our senior officer,
Desmond "Bejeezes" Piers, in the destroyer, *Restigouche,*
about the upcoming revels.

Eventually, the principal guest showed up, the dark outline
of the big battleship looming out of the fog. But she was
ahead of schedule; the Americans had neglected to shift onto
local Newfoundland time, and weren't expecting Winston's
lot for another hour and a half. Accordingly, the PM and
whole platoons of politicans and top brass had to pace up

and down outside in cold dudgeon while their hosts finished the breakfast dishes and got everything ready. Promptly at nine a.m. *Prince of Wales* showed up again on the doormat and was welcomed in, and since she came with even more destroyers, we thankfully handed over our screening chores and went inside to join the party.

And quite a party it was, with bugles and bands all over the lot. The big marine band aboard *Prince of Wales* played "The Star Strangled Banner", as Bill Harvey insisted on calling it, and *Augusta*'s band responded with "The King". Winnie waved the V-sign across the narrowing gap between the ships, and Roosevelt gave him the famous big smile, complete with jaunty cigarette holder, and sent a boat loaded with cigarettes and other goodies from peacetime America for the crew of *Prince of Wales*. The contrast between war and peace, between rationed austerity and peaceful plenty, was apparent in the ships themselves. The *Prince* was dark and somber, her brass painted over; the U.S. ships sparkled with bright brass and white decks, and at night—miracle of miracles—they shone with light. It was incredible to realize that this could be done safely here; with a feeling of something like guilt we opened our own scuttles and black-out screens to let the cool fresh air in and the light out to shine on the dark water. It was a strange, dreamlike interlude in the dark ordeal of war.

Although she carried Winston and a regiment of top brass, it was the *Prince of Wales* herself who was the hit of our show. She was then the most modern battleship afloat, and we couldn't wait to get aboard for a look over her. Fortunately, Ralph Ripley, a former great Varsity quarterback and a friend of ours, was serving aboard as a junior—very junior!—radar officer, and we wangled an invitation to lunch, and were duly impressed as Ralph led us on a tour of her electronic marvels, blinding us with science at every turn.

She was vast and complex, infinitely sophisticated, but she lacked the brute strength, the sense of primeval power that we'd felt in *Rodney*. We were awed by the ingenuity and intricacy of *Prince of Wales*' control systems, but all the same their very complexity made one slightly uneasy. In the stress of war, simple things are best; we'd learned to distrust some of this over-sensitive electronic gear, which always seemed to pack up when it was most needed, and we gathered from Ralph that the *Prince*'s teething troubles, which had so humiliated her in her brush with *Bismarck* before she was properly worked up, had still not been completely resolved.

It seemed significant, somehow, that when the crunch came half the marvellous gear aboard *Prince of Wales* collapsed in a shower of sparks and blue flame, while the simple, straightforward slugging power of the *Rodney* shot great chunks out of *Bismarck*.

Still, for simple country boys fresh from a corvette, the *Prince* was strictly Buck Rogers stuff, and we enjoyed her hugely, so much so that the following morning, a Sunday, we were happy to return with church parties sent over by each ship for the elaborate services to be held on *Prince of Wales'* vast quarterdeck. Like everyone else, we goggled at all the bigwigs sitting in chairs in the front row, along with Franklin Roosevelt and Winston Churchill, or immediately behind; there was a good bit of shuffling about among the luminaries to get themselves into a position befitting their rank and status, a kind of gold-laced version of the navy's old evolution of "tallest on left, shortest on right, *size!*" Between hymns, there was a good deal of surreptitious whispering as onlookers tried to identify the more prominent of the many personalities here assembled; was that dyspeptic really Admiral King, and if that fellow who looks a little like Joe E. Brown is General Marshall, who's the little runt in air-force braid and buttons? There were all our own chiefs of staff, of course—Dill and Pound and Freeman, Cherwell and Cadogan—but the President had brought a group of civilians with him whom we recognized from old copies of *Life* magazine: Harry Hopkins and Sumner Welles and Averell Harriman, as well as his own armed forces chiefs. One way or another, it seemed that all the principal talents, political and military, of the western world had been assembled on the quarterdeck of this tremendous ship, anchored in total wilderness completely isolated from the civilized world beyond. Everybody present was keenly aware of the historical significance of this occasion, that this meeting of powers was unique in our time and obviously of the greatest consequence to the future course of world events.

Everybody that is, except for the two chaplains, one British, the other American. Between them, they conducted one of the most interminably tedious services it has ever been my misfortune to have to squirm through. Neither seemed to have any concept of the uniqueness, the significance, of the occasion, neither conceded so much as a passing reference to the great events here in train. Instead, we prayed for every-one and everything under the sun: for politicians, great and small, and for all the usual intangibles so dear to the hearts of clergymen—wisdom and peace and understanding, etc. On and on they droned, while the matelots in the back rows fid-geted and sucked their teeth, and even Winston seemed restless. It was a frightful bore, but it was enlivened by two rousing hymns, chosen, as it later appeared, by the PM him-self. We all stood and roared out "O God, Our Help in Ages Past", which seemed to draw both Yanks and Limeys into some common cause, and we closed out the service with a real rouser, "Onward, Christian Soldiers". The marine band really laid into this one, and everyone seemed to sort of catch the spirit: at the final, "On, then, Christian soldiers, on to vic-tory!" Winnie was waving his hand about like an orchestra conductor, and all the bluejackets were shouting at the top of their voices. We all ended up out of breath but with a feeling that we'd somehow accomplished something. Score one for Winston.

Afterward the band marched itself off with a rousing quickstep, and all the hundreds of visitors found their way down into the boats lined up alongside to return to their ships. But Debbie Piers, our senior officer, gathered some of the officers from his group under his wing and led the way into the *Prince of Wales'* cavernous wardroom. Here Roose-velt and Winston were holding court in a circle of admirals, generals, and air marshals, with mere captains and command-ers scrambling around the fringes trying to catch a glimpse of the great men in their midst.

It was here that Piers showed his mettle. Whatever his other virtues as escort commander—and we had sailed with lots worse—he was second to none on the social circuit, and not one to be put off by a parcel of over-age soldiers who'd picked up their limited social graces sipping bourbon and branchwater at some sun-baked camp in Kansas. Elbowing his way through all the heavy brass, Debbie approached the Great Man, interrupting Winston in mid-sentence; would they, he inquired, like to meet the officers of their escort, the men who brought them here? It was one of those questions which had only one answer; in no time at all we were lined up, furtively wiping our palms on our trouser legs, and intro-duced one by one to each of these demi-gods, with Piers do-ing the honours and each of us being treated to a warm handshake and a bright smile.

Afterward we were led away in a kind of daze, and gulped restoratives in a quiet corner, eyed, rather irritably it seemed to us, by legions of regular service officers, whose red faces and gold lace attested to their vast seniority. That a clutch of whey-faced colonials, probably milk-drinkers to a man, with only a spindly single band of lace on their cuffs, should have hob-nobbed with the Lord's anointed, and in *their* wardroom, obviously galled them. And when they caught sight of Jackson's red lapel-patch, you could see them blench: a grubby-collared reserve midshipman, the lowest form of pond life, normally tolerated only in some smelly gunroom; were they to be spared nothing?

The atmosphere becoming distinctly oppressive, we were glad to take our departure, walking, it seemed, about six inches above the deck. In the boat home, we broke into hilarious chatter, elated by our glimpse of greatness, and traded reminiscences of what FDR had said to this one of us, or what Winston had said to that. Jackson, the lone midshipman in our midst, vowed that he would not wash his right hand until the war's end; the hand that had shaken those of President and Prime Minister, he felt, should be preserved in its pristine condition. However, he later withdrew his vow when it was pointed out to him, perhaps unkindly, that snotties' personal habits being what they were, his gesture was likely to go quite unnoticed among his seniors in the wardroom. But we knew just how he felt; all of us could hardly wait to get a letter off home, and for years we could draw all eyes at the bar when we began a conversation with: "The last time I chatted with Winston . . ." or "Franklin told me himself . . ."

For us, after that, all was anti-climax. Even the ringing phrases of the Atlantic Charter with its lofty delineation of human rights, the coping-stone of the Atlantic Alliance drawn up at Argentia, failed to impress men who were, so to speak, personally acquainted with the President of the United States and the Prime Minister of Great Britian.

We were patrolling the approaches when the *Prince of Wales* sailed past us on her journey home; we watched her fade into the evening twilight, tall and sombre and majestic. It was to be the last time that any of us would see her. . . .

Curiously, the news of her sinking, not so many months later, thrown away with *Repulse* by an admiral's miscalculation, an error obvious to the merest middy, seemed shocking but not really surprising. For the truth was that *Prince of*

Wales was a loser; in all we had heard of her, seen of her, she appeared to be a kind of lemon. Ships take on character and personality by some indefinable process; some ships— *Warspite, Cossack, Rodney,* our own *Haida*— "had it"; others, somehow, did not. *Prince of Wales* was tarred with the ignominy of failure from the first, when she was hustled into a confrontation with the world's most formidable warship before she was operationally ready. Her crew untrained, her armament and equipment untried, and with gangs of civilian dockyard workers still aboard trying to complete installations of turrets even as they were being trained on the enemy, she failed to avenge her consort after *Hood* blew up, and was forced to draw off with some of *Bismarck's* shrapnel in her. She had been humiliated, through no real fault of her own, and unlike the rest of her class she never really achieved a success. We thought that at Argentina she was sloppy and unimpressive for a flagship carrying so many distinguished passengers; that enormous crew should have been able to lick her into better shape for such an occasion.

Her loss didn't move us; what really shook us was the loss of so many friends, new and old, and particularly Ralph Ripley, surely the nearest thing to an All-Canadian Boy our generation produced. A star athlete at school and university, he was a fine scholar and leader of men; we were proud to be his friend. In the Royal Navy, as in any human institution, error was inevitable, but the damage entailed was fearful. For as Kipling remarked, blood is the price of admiralty, and the RN paid it, bravely and unstintingly. Sometimes, as with the *Prince of Wales,* the price was just too high.

Yet it was the Royal Navy itself which wrote the noblest epitaph to Ripley, and to all the other young men of every commonwealth country who went down with its ships. On the Royal Navy's memorial on Plymouth Hoe, where all their names are listed, thousand upon thousand, is the Biblical text: "All these were honoured of their generation, and were the glory of their times."

8
THE CRUEL SEA

~~~~~~

They brought *Candytuft* slowly up the harbour, leaning heavily on the tugs alongside, like an injured player being assisted from the field of play, and berthed her at the ramshackle jetty on the South Side of St. John's. It was there that we visited her later in the afternoon, filled with horror and speaking in low voices as one did in the presence of the dead. There was nothing markedly wrong with her appearance above decks, apart from a marked list, but there was something ghastly about her for all of that. It was her silence, for one thing, and the darkness that wrapped about her deserted messdecks; the ship was absolutely still, with the silence of the dead, without the background hum of fans, the myriad vibrations of busy machinery, which in a ship is the breath of life. Somewhere deep in her bowels a clang reverberated through her, as the shore party probed her inky depths for what they dreaded to find; long power cables snaked from the shore down her stokehold hatch to light them on their way.

But it was the stench that was the ultimate horror—the smell of cooked meat, somehow faintly familiar and odiously appetizing, that pervaded the ship and hung over her jetty; she was like an enormous stew-pot that had cooked her crew in her own superheated steam. In shocked silence we watched from the wharf while the remains, wrapped in blankets and held together in basket stretchers, were winched up from her blackened stokehold, her blistered wardroom flat, her peeling cabins and corridors. *Candytuft* had experienced the ultimate terror, the nightmare that disturbs the slumber of thousands of young sailors, sleeping for the first time among the pulsating pipes and hot fittings of a crowded steamship. Aboard

Candytuft, the nightmare we had learned to ignore had come true; her boilers had collapsed and engulfed her sleepers in a burning cloud of live steam. A mechanical failure, an inattentive stoker, and suddenly a disciplined and purposeful man-of-war screening the flanks of an Atlantic convoy had been transformed into a hissing, scorching hell, where helpless men went shrieking to their deaths in clouds of burning steam. The exploding boilers had carved in the great bulkhead separating the stokehold from the wardroom flat and the officers' cabins, flooding the space with superheated steam and killing men as they slept.

Later, in the lime-washed serenity of a hospital ward, *Candytuft*'s young midshipman told us how it had been on that fearful night, his cheerful, fresh young face at odds with his bandaged hands, enormous as baseball mitts, which lay above the blankets. He had been asleep when the boilers had gone, he told us, but had been awakened in his bunk by the noise of the explosion and the collapsing bulkhead. Dazed as he was, he had yet had the remarkable presence of mind to dive beneath the blankets when the first wave of live steam had come shrieking into the flat, and to stay there until the all-engulfing cloud had passed. Wild with terror, he had emerged later to find that the burning steam had risen to the deckhead above, forming a thick and growing layer overhead. He had tumbled out just as the lights died, leaving the ship in darkness save for the faint blue glow of the emergency lighting. Realizing that he would have to make his escape immediately or be trapped in his cabin by the ever-lowering cloud of steam above him, he wrapped himself in a blanket and made for the door. Peering out into the dim-lit alleyway, he found it running deep in scalding water; in his bare feet, he could never have made it to the ladder leading to the upper deck and outer air. It was then that this fresh-faced youngster, the cheerful companion of many of our pleasant runs ashore, showed what he was capable of. With incredible coolness, he had turned back into his cabin, crouched beneath the burning cloud overhead, and rummaged in a locker for his seaboots. He'd pulled them on and then, wrapping his blanket completely over his head and face and body, he had plunged out the door, down the alleyway, and up through the fearful layer of live steam and out into the cool darkness and safety of the upper deck. He had forgotten only his hands; clutching the blanket tight about him, they had been exposed to the terrible heat of the steam as he had fought his way up through

it, and they had suffered fearfully. Swollen into gross caricatures of human appendages, they had driven him nearly mad
with pain; a quick-thinking officer injected an ampoule of
pain-killer from the ship's emergency kit, and doctors, afloat
and ashore, had fought to save them. Now, propped up
against the pillows, he used them to hold a paper cup to his
chest as he sucked fruit juice from a straw and re-lived the
terrible night which had taken the lives of so many of his
shipmates.

Towed back to port with her survivors and her dead, *Candytuft* lived to sail again; hers had been a freak accident. A
more common cause of trouble to wartime ocean escorts was
the North Atlantic weather, particularly in wintertime. By
shore standards, the usual weather prevailing over most of the
North Atlantic is frightful; the sun is rarely seen, obscured by
the heavy cloud cover typical of the area, the temperature is
rarely warm, and the winds, especially the prevailing wester-
lies, are damp and cold and boisterous. But it was the com-
paratively tiny size of corvettes that made them especially
vulnerable to the weather. Seamen who had traded across the
Atlantic all their lives in merchant ships discovered for the
first time just how important a factor weather was to life in
the North Atlantic, stripped of the insulation afforded by the
size of one's ship. In a corvette, the level of the main deck in
the waist is only a foot or two above the surface of the sea,
so that almost any sort of wave is high enough to wash down
her decks and send broken water over her upper-works. For
much of her time at sea, a corvette was, for all practical purposes, semi-submerged, her fo'c'sle swept by any head sea,
her well-decks perpetually awash, and her superstructure
bombarded by flying spray, up to and over the height of her
bridge and funnel.

Yet while they were exceptionally lively, rolling and
pitching in the slightest sea, corvettes were remakable sea-
boats coming to no harm in conditions which damaged or
overwhelmed their larger sisters. Theirs was the immunity of
the cork, forever bobbing about on the surface but escaping
the worst blows of even the most furious seas.

There were, of course, pleasant days, fine weather, even in
the winter, but these were interludes, to be cherished in
memory after being savoured to the full. Generally speaking,
life at sea in a corvette was cold and wet and miserable, with
constant violent motion and a background of noise compounded of whistling wind, bashing hull, rattling and clanging

fittings, surging and gurgling water. The world outside was perpetually grey; sea, horizon, clouds, even the light itself had a dingy look.

And yet, curiously enough, for all its misery and hardship in really bad weather, life in the corvettes was happy enough at sea. One can grow used to anything, and once you grew accustomed to the incessant motion life settled into a routine. Off-watch in the messdecks men slept incessantly in the really bad weather, shutting out the appalling sights and sounds beyond the blankets, but at other times they read and joked and played cards. In the wardroom, we played an endless game of Blackjack night and day, into which watch-keepers plunged on leaving the bridge. Everyone's score was kept track of in a battered scribbler, and although nobody ever paid off, and it was understood that real cash was not involved, the accumulated debts most of us picked up on paper used to reach such appalling levels that by general consent there would be a devaluation, with debts being reassessed at ten cents on the dollar, and the game could start again.

Even Percy, our ship's groundhog mascot, quickly settled into a comfortable shipboard routine. I had been deputized to bring back a mascot, preferably a parrot, for our refitting ship while on leave in Toronto. We were currently under the spell of a consort's parrot, which used to shuffle about the rim of the wardroom table and screech, "Where's father?" followed by a *sotto voce* muttering of "The old bugger! The old bugger!" But in downtown Toronto I had seen this incredible groundhog, following along at the heels of its owner through all the crowds of a noonday Yonge Street lunch-hour, and knew instantly that this was for us. This particular animal, it transpired, belonged to Mr. Skinner, who ran a famous pet-shop in the old Arcade. She was not for sale, but she had a litter of pups back in the store and I bought one on the spot, a toothy little devil no bigger than a squirrel, and arranged for him to be shipped out to us in a box packed with cabbage leaves to sustain his considerable appetite.

He arrived in Newfyjohn in splendid shape, and popped out of his box and sat up on the magazine hatch in the wardroom flat and ate his first sea-biscuit, watched by an admiring throng. He was an ideal mascot; quickly housebroken to a sandbox, which he used like a cat, he dearly loved to play. He went about dragging an old glove, which he offered to everyone in the hope that they would play with him, trying to take it from him as one does with a puppy, while he grunted in mimic fury. He became an adept climber, and would whistle up the wardroom curtain like a cat, or shinny up a voice-pipe if one was foolish enough to take him on the bridge for company, as I was sometimes known to do.

Percy was supposed to live in the cabin flat aft, or in the wardroom, since he was grossly over-fed if he ventured into the galley or the fo'c'sle; he knew this well enough, but he was as cunning as a fox. From the bridge wing, I would see his furry head appear over the coaming of the after flat; two beady eyes would check that the coast was clear. Then, waiting for the outboard roll—for he was as sea-wise as any shell-backed sailor and knew that the waist would clear itself of water as the ship rolled outward—he would leap out onto the wet deck and scuttle like mad for the galley, reaching the sanctuary of its lower step before the next sea came toppling inboard.

Percy survived many vicissitudes—his seagoing diet was notably short of the green grass staple of his shoreside chums—but his most notable triumph of adjustment occurred when he grew overly curious while spying on the engineer's storekeeper and fell down the storeroom hatch. He broke both his big front upper teeth on the steel deck; after vainly gumming his usual cabbage leaf that night, he huddled miserably in a corner in a snit. Nor would he eat the long strips of leaf we cut up for him; we thought he was doomed.

But a remarkable thing happened. His lower teeth, now unopposed by the dominant upper teeth, grew with incredible rapidity, and in no time Percy was nibbling away, as good as new—but now he was undershot, instead of overshot, and so he remained.

Life at sea went on happily enough; it was only when things got a bit "bumpy" that conditions became unendurable. A real North Atlantic gale, viewed from a liner's deck, can be merely unpleasant; in a battened-down corvette, tossed about like a cork, it can try men to the limits. A winter crossing was an endless succession of gales that came shrieking down from the western Arctic; we would no sooner emerge thankfully from one when the next would engulf us. Ferocious winter weather became a part of the experience of everyone in the escort navy; what lived on in memory were the one or two "ultimate storms" which brought home to everyone the enormous, incomprehensible force and fury of the sea. No corvette sailor ever talked of "ruling the waves" or "conquering the deep"; he knew from experience that man crept across the vastness of the oceans, a microcosm in the grasp of forces immeasurably greater than anything he could muster. He learned that man survived, after all his own efforts had been expended, by luck or fate or destiny, or by the Hand of God; take your pick. But no man could go back to sea without a sense of fatalism after once having experienced its incalculable force; a force that could engulf great ships, or crush the stoutest steel bulkhead, as it did when it crumpled the entire forward structure on a four-stack destroyer, killing its captain as he lay in his bunk. The ocean, like outer space, is an element beyond human comprehension, an expression of the infinite power and immensity of the universe.

We experienced its awesome strength in Decembr 1941, heading south from Iceland to pick up and escort a westbound convoy; five corvettes led by the destroyer *Restigouche*. It was snowing when we left Hvalfjord, and as we emerged into the open ocean we went pitching into a full gale, which grew worse hour by hour. By nightfall, when we had still not found our ships, things were getting desperate; we had no radar, and to run into a convoy under such conditions could be disastrous. We turned onto the likely course of the convoy and ran along, hoping to see something before it hit us, our ships spread in line abreast, a mile apart.

In the shrieking blackness of the night, the wind rose steadily as the barometer dropped; by midnight it had passed hurricane force and we could only estimate its strength at over a hundred miles an hour. The world went mad; the snow and sleet, mixed with spray, drove horizontally over the water. No man could face that blast; we doubled our watches, so that one officer could shelter behind the asdic house for a moment before relieving the other crouched behind the canvas bridge dodger, over which he had to snatch a glimpse into the shrieking maelstrom ahead. The seas grew and grew under the frightful impetus of the wind; by midnight they were mountainous, and after that nobody bothered to contemplate their height and weight. They blotted out our world, towering above us in the darkness, shutting off the wind for a breathless moment before thundering down upon us. Miraculously the bows would rise, so that only the top of the sea would come crashing inboard, to sweep across our fo'c'sle and thunder against our bridge and funnel. Everything small or frail had long been swept away by the seas breaking over us; winch covers, vent screens, rope reels. Each mountain that came towering out of the darkness, its crest outlined in luminous foam, would seem to be the last we could survive; peering up at its ghastly immensity, our hearts would sink and, bowing our heads, we would commit ourselves to whatever power watched over us. "O God, help us! Help us!" The captain huddled, grey-faced, beside the officers rotating on watch; nobody spoke, or could have spoken, in the howling madness of wind and sleet and driven spray. Nobody doubted that it must end, one way or another, within the hour; either the hurricane must pass or the ship would break up and be overwhelmed.

It went on, day and night, for four days.

By noon on the second day we were mindless automatons, so numbed mentally and physically by the incessant violence of our world as to have become inured. We no longer cared whether we lived or died; it seemed no longer to concern us. But for all of that, life went on within the beaten hulls of our ships; watches changed, men ate a little and slept as best they could in the frightful din of the hurricane. We had been washed bare of everything on the upper deck; the Carley floats gone, the whaler stove in, but still our ship lived.

Late on the afternoon of the second day, *Restigouche* began to break up. Her mast went overside, her steering gear broke down, her fragile hull long, and vulnerable, began to open up. Her depth-charges were battered from their lashings and swept overside; steering as best she could with her twin propellers, she became a wave-swept wreck. By nightfall she had turned tail to wind and was running desperately before the storm, struggling to stay afloat, with more than six feet of water in her lower compartments. She vanished swiftly from our ken; four days later she crawled, what was left of her, into Greenock.

Left on our own, we punched mindlessly on. On the third day, a signal from the commodore gave our convoy's position as some thirty miles away, and hove to; we crept towards them but by nightfall we, too, were forced to heave to, barely able to maintain our position by steaming slowly into the tempest. Our convoy had become secondary; now our main concern was to survive.

None of us, later, could remember the events of that storm; all the hours, the agonies, the anxieties of those days and nights became telescoped in memory into a blurred recollection of a single experience. But on the fourth day the sky lightened, became patchy; the wind dropped away with miraculous speed. Within hours only the mountainous seas were left to remind us of what we had endured, and apart from the superficial damage to our upper decks, all our corvettes were afloat and sound and fighting fit; we had survived!

Years later, caught by a similar hurricane south of Cape Canso, we were not so fortunate. This time we were on the continental shelf, which heightens and steepens the seas over it, and so far to the westward that the temperature dropped below freezing, a rarity in mid-ocean. To make things worse, the wind veered quickly to put Sable Island, that nightmarish ships' graveyard, under our lee. We could not afford to turn our little convoy of ships, unladen and therefore riding high and vulnerable to the force of the wind, and run before the tempest.

Early in the storm, we lost our "monkey island"; a great sea, a "seventh wave" even taller than the rest, simply engulfed us, blotting out bridge and funnel in green water. There was a tremendous crash, and when the sea passed, our asdic house had been stripped bare of the little wooden bridge we had built on top of it; miraculously Nels Adams, the watch-keeper, was still there, clutching the exposed voice-pipe and grinning down at us.

But the seas were not themselves our greatest danger; our chief menace was the ice that each one left behind, and that enveloped us in a rapidly thickening coat of marble-hard frozen spray. In an hour we had acquired tons of heavy ice on our masts and superstructure, top-weight which made the ship unstable. In no time the ship began to lie over, to recover more slowly each time she rolled; if something was not done, and done quickly, we must inevitably roll over as the weight of our upper-works upset our normal stability.

Everyone in the ship was mustered ready, with something—anything—hard enough and heavy enough to hammer ice. At a word from the captain, the ship turned, rolled agonizingly in the trough, but recovered—just—and then we were running before the storm, the wind and sea whistling behind, and we were into a new and tolerable world. Instantly, everyone was set to work chopping, hacking, hammering at the foot-thick casing of ice that had built up over bridge and rails and boats, masts and rigging. It was desperate, wearying work; the ice was so hard, and there was so much of it. A steam hose was rigged by the stokers, and melted some of the more difficult patches; the atmosphere aboard was one of frantic, desperate effort, for we all knew that we could only run before the storm for a brief time, with the shoals of Sable Island so close in our lee.

In half an hour we had rid ourselves of the worst of it. Her motion now restored to normal, the ship swung back to her old course, and we were plunged again into the shrieking hurricane, the driving spray, the freezing cold. Three times the ship iced heavily; three times we put our stern to it and cleared ourselves of the ice that clawed our ship over and down.

Our ships in convoy were not so fortunate, their long hulls, riding high in the water, were unmanageable in the frightful wind. The convoy dispersed, disintegrated, as each ship steered as best it could. In the grey light of a stormy dawn, I sighted the rescue ship, a little coastal passenger vessel that had once carried holiday-makers to British resorts; from her bridge a red Aldis lamp began to blink a signal to us. A great sea intervened, blotting her from sight; when it passed, she was nowhere to be seen. She had simply been engulfed, and weighted down with ice, had sunk in an instant.

During that day and night we lost three other merchantmen, great, ocean-going ships that had accumulated such enormous weights of ice that they had simply toppled over and been engulfed by the tremendous seas. Their crews were too small, in that freezing blast, to remove the vast areas of ice, and their hulls were too long for the ships, encumbered as they were, to be manoeuvred in the giant sea. All of them sank like a stone; we survivors, merchantmen and escorts alike, were powerless to lift a finger to help.

Yet one of our ships was destined to have a miraculous experience. Helpless and listing beneath a great weight of ice, she had driven before the storm down to leeward, her propeller churning away but unable to steer herself in the grip of that overwhelming wind and sea. Soon, the horrified crew saw the sea white with breakers ahead, a line of white surf stretching right across the horizon. They were driving down onto the shoals of Sable Island, the monstrous seas breaking furiously on the long scimitar of sand that rose from the ocean depths. As the ship drove toward the sands, both anchors were let go, bringing her bows around to face the wind. The anchors held momentarily, then dragged, then held. Little by little, the ship was driven remorselessly backward to her doom, the anchors slowing her progress but unable to get a firm hold in the shifting sands of the great shoal.

It was then that the miracle occurred. There is a shallow

passage, a sort of lagoon, dividing Sable Island from its outlying shoals. The ship was driven by the storm, stern first, through this passage, so that she literally went right through Sable Island to emerge, unscathed, on the other side! In the sudden calm of the island's lee, she anchored peacefully and rode out the rest of the storm in the shelter of Sable itself.

But we had other enemies besides the weather in the North Atlantic. The memories of anyone who served in the escort ships are filled with torpedoings, and the survivors who were the inevitable aftermath of ship sinkings. Nobody who has ever seen human beings struggling for life in the sea can ever doubt the common brotherhood of man; there is an intangible, unspoken bond that links the struggling survivor, battling for life against all the immensity of wind and sea, with the watchers on the ship, a bond that reaches to the very heart of the beholder, so that the swimmer's fight, his fate, become our own. A man swimming in the sea seems unbelievably tiny, lost amid the vastness of the ocean about him; to rescue him from that uncaring immensity seems somehow a triumph of the human spirit against the ordered anonymity of the universe encompassing us. Those sodden, shivering, oil-smothered wretches dragged inboard and restored to the warmth of our messdecks from the darkness of the midnight ocean had been snatched back from the abyss that awaits us all; they had the glazed look of men who had been carried to the outer limits of human experience, and had glimpsed the face of Destiny.

Tales of such men, of those who lived, those who died, filled the reminiscences of corvette crews ashore. There was the haunting story of men plucked in good health and spirit, from a sinking ship by the escort *Minas*. Not long after they had been taken aboard, a couple of men began to cough, to struggle, to fall into delirium. In a matter of minutes they lay dead, and it was only then that talk began about the cargo their ship had been carrying: containers of poison gas for storage in the U.K. for retaliatory use in the event of a Nazi gas attack. Somehow, the torpedoing had loosed some of this fearful gas. Into the eyes of the remaining survivors came the look of dawning realization as coughing began among still others—they were all doomed. Within hours the last one lay cold and stiff. *Minas*, who had rescued a joyous party of live survivors, steamed on with a cargo of corpses.

Our own particular horror concerned the survivors of the American troopship *Chatham*, carrying workers to the new

air base at Thule in Greenland. The ship had been torpedoed
by the redoubtable Hartwig in U517, the U-boat that
wrought so much damage and heartache in the Gulf of St.
Lawrence in the summer of 1942, and we were detached
from the escort of a nearby convoy to rescue a couple of
boatloads of survivors in Belle Isle strait. They were in good
shape when we found them; like most American lifeboats,
their boats had more gear, and certainly better gear, than we
carried in our ship. But lying amongst them on a blanket
stained with blood and oil was a man obviously badly injured; we passed him carefully inboard, and took him forward to be worked on.

In our crowded messdeck, our sick-berth attendant and I,
as first lieutenant, did our best to save him. We would never
forget the horror which awaited us when we cut away his
clothes. He had been so badly crushed that he was just a sort
of pudding; there seemed to be no bone unbroken, nothing to
give human shape to this frightfully mangled mass. And yet
he lived; we killed his pain with novocaine, did our best to
make him comfortable. I wiped away the oil from his mouth
and eyes; strangely, I could not seem to wipe his face clean
of the greasy black. It was only when, puzzled, I bent close to
examine his poor face that I realized that I had been attempting to wipe a Negro white. Thank God he died quickly and
peacefully; crushed beneath a heavy raft falling from the ship
above him after he had jumped overside, he was the most
fearfully injured man I had ever seen alive.

But Hartwig and U517 had yet more horrors for us. Asdic
conditions in northern gulf waters were hopeless for the asdic
sets we then possessed; the mixing of salt water with fresh, of
cold water with warm, where the vast St. Lawrence empties
into the cold North Atlantic, produced a "layering" effect
which bounced back transmissions from our asdic sets,
masking the submarine beneath. Hartwig soon sensed his immunity from normal detection in these waters, and made the
most of it. He was destined to sink several more vessels, including our chummy ship, *Shawinigan,* before being sunk
himself by aircraft from the carrier *Victorious.* But on this
particular night, he closed our convoy as we entered the
Strait of Belle Isle, bound north with supplies for the new air
base at Goose Bay on the Labrador coast. The corvette *Weyburn,* on the far side of the little convoy, spotted the wash of
his conning tower, but as she turned to attack, Hartwig got

away a torpedo which hit the old lake steamer *Donald Stewart*, loaded with airplanes and high-test gasoline.

While *Weyburn* went after Hartwig, we closed the stricken ship. A boatload of survivors managed to get away and were picked up by the ship astern, but no sooner had they left the ship's side than there was a tremendous explosion, and a vast column of flame towered up into the night sky. The high-octane gasoline had exploded, and the burning ship became a sheet of flame from stem to stern, lighting up the scene for miles around. A wave of burning gasoline poured overside; in seconds, the ship was floating on a sea of flame, burning as fiercely as did the ship herself. We closed the scene, appalled by the sight and sound of that frightful inferno, for the roaring suction of the air rushing in to fill that column of fire was deafening.

It was then that the thing happened that was to haunt our dreams ever afterward. A door in the after house of the doomed ship opened, and out stepped a man clad for a city street, in topcoat and hat, and carrying a small suitcase. He looked about him, first at the roaring inferno just forward, then at the sea of flame overside. Then, with no sign of alarm or despair, he turned and stepped back into the cabin flat inside, closing the door carefully behind him. We never saw him again; within minutes the *Donald Stewart* slid her red-hot length beneath the waves, bearing with her her lone passenger.

Who he was we never learned, but the horror of his situation, with death closing in on him from every side, cutting off every avenue of escape, was more than we could bear. The cool and calm acceptance of his fate by that unknown man, so close that we could see his every feature, yet already on the doorstep of eternity, we have never forgotten, can never forget.

Perhaps the blackest moment in the escort navy was the introduction of the acoustic torpedo in the fall of 1943. Two convoy escort forces and a support group, gathered about a single enormous fleet made up of two convoys combined, had been assaulted by a swarm of U-boats using the new weapon and new tactics, attacking the escorts, rather than the merchantmen. The frigate *Lagan*, hot in pursuit of one U-boat, had been torpedoed by another, the shattering explosion blowing off thirty feet of her stern. *St. Croix* was next; the old four-piper, so familar to everyone on the Newfy-Derry run, was shattered and sunk by no fewer than three torpedoes right aft while investigating a contact; most of her crewmen survived the explosion, but were left clinging to rafts in the freezing water for thirteen long hours.

The fatal delay was the result of another disaster; the corvette Polyanthus, one of a pair known as "the Anthus sisters, Poly and Di", was sent to pick them up, but she never arrived. She was torpedoed astern and perished in a single great explosion, taking down with her all save one of her men. He, and eighty-five of St. Croix's numbed survivors, were taken aboard the frigate Itchen. It was the next night when the greatest tragedy occurred; Itchen, loaded with survivors, switching her searchlight on to a surfaced U-boat dead ahead of the convoy, simply disappeared in a tremendous mushroom-topped pillar of flame, torpedoed in her propellers. Only three men survived of more than two hundred aboard; one from Itchen, one from St. Croix, and the survivor from Polyanthus.

The surviving ships of the groups berthing in Newfyjohn were badly shaken; the stories they told us in their normally cheerful wardrooms were full of foreboding. Obviously, Hitler had launched one of his vaunted "secret weapons", and no one was sure that anybody could devise a counter to this dreaded killer, which homed on the noise of a ship's propellers. Yet within days the acoustic torpedo had been reduced to mere nuisance value, first by the issue of "foxer" gear by the Admiralty, and later with our own, better, simpler "cat" (counter-acoustic torpedo) gear; a couple of short lengths of pipe, clamped together side by side close enough to clang incessantly when towed through the water at the end of a long wire, and thus making enough racket to attract any acoustic torpedo away from the lesser noise of the ship's propellers.

The attrition of ships and men went on, month after month, year after year, regardless of the ups and downs of Allied fortunes; in the family of the escort navy, each casualty in the groups removed a familiar household, a distinctive group of characters, a particular friend. The bitterest to bear were the lives lost that could have been, should have been saved; Valleyfield's men, 115 of them, dying in the bergstrewn waters while other ships of her group blundered unknowingly about close by; the long ordeal of Guyborough's men when the bitter sea swallowed up my old shipmate Tommy Holland and so many others, victims of a staff officer's error.

Awe, and fear, of the ocean grew on everyone who sailed over it, winter and summer, year after year. The ultimate bliss in our lives was to escape from the sea for a time to the haven of a refit port, where the ship would be taken in hand for repairs and alterations, and where her ship's company could go off on long leave. In theory a ship was refitted every twelve months; in practice, particularly in the early years when escorts were scarce, it might be eighteen months to two years. But eventually the time would come when we would be ordered to refit, and we could all go home for up to twenty-eight days. Leave, of course, was the big thing; the return to a normal, civilized world, far from the war and the sea, was the great restorative, although home always seemed just a little different from the way one had remembered it. One's parents seemed a little older, a little greyer; the house a little smaller, one's old clothes and books and belongings just a bit naive, a trifle juvenile. But it was wonderful to wander the old familiar streets, to toss a baseball or football about with a kid brother, to learn from the hometown paper and friends how well we were winning the war.

Even on returning to the ship, there was the pleasure in being part of the life of a small community, if you were lucky enough to have been sent to refit in one of those innumerable pleasant little sunlit ports that dot the river-mouths of the Maritimes: Liverpool or Lunenburg, Pictou or Dalhousie or Shelburne. The ship was a chaotic mess of plumbers and painters and riveters, of course, and life aboard during working hours nearly impossible, but you could escape ashore to the pleasant tree-lined streets, the comfortable homes and hospitable people of these most charming of towns.

Life there was never dull. Who could forget Black Maggie, the redoubtable widow who carried on her late husband's coal business with such flair, or the afternoon a guest of hers, an air-force group captain, no less, got out on her roof, for reasons remembered now only by himself, and clambered up to the roof edge, only to find on arriving there that the roof was so steep he could not bring himself to descend it? He sat there, in full uniform, while passersby gathered below, some to shout advice and others, sad to say, to jeer and jest at this gallant officer. Certainly a diverting spectacle, and one that quite made our day; we were sorry when the volunteer fire brigade, with a long record behind them of rescuing tabbies from trees, arrived to add a group captain to their bag.

It was in the same town that I was put in charge of a naval contingent, drawn from the ship's companies of two corvettes refitting there, to march in a Victory Loan parade. We were all duly fallen in on the schoolground marshalling area. As the representatives of the Senior Service, we were of course intent on securing our privileged place at the head of the parade, leaving the army trainees and air-force cadets to scramble for places behind along with assorted Boy Scouts, policemen, our old friends of the fire brigade, and anyone else who could find a uniform to wear. We were duly getting ourselves shaped up, dressing our ranks, shouldering arms, and forming columns of route and that sort of thing, when the band began to step out, playing a jaunty tune. And we were about to move off, in proper marching order, when a crowd of Brownies behind us grew impatient at what they seemed to think was our procrastination. With a simple, single command. "Come along, girls," their bespectacled leader (The Big Brownie? The Brown Lady?) shepherded her tittering flock right past us in the wake of the band, leaving us to follow, at our slow, navy pace in the No. 2 spot. It was a lesson we never forgot; in manoeuvring large numbers of men, or a gaggle of sparrow-legged girls, simplicity of commands is the essence.

Those idyllic interludes in tiny refit ports were so many rays of sunshine in the grim, grey world of the wartime North Atlantic.

9
THEM AND US

A dominant factor of life in the escort fleet was the "them and us" mentality, which separated the crews of ships from their Canadian counterparts ashore. Partly, this was engendered by the sense of shared experience which bound crews and groups in a common brotherhood, an experience it was impossible to explain or rationalize ashore. The truth was that almost every convoy crossing was an ordeal so gruelling that, once experienced, nothing could induce a repetition of its agonies; nothing, that is, save pride. Pride of ship and service and group, but mainly pride of toughness, of being one of a select company which could face up, again and again, to the terrors and hardships of a North Atlantic winter. It was the same pride, surely, that sustained men in the trenches in the First World War, and produced a similar sense of comradeship.

When we came ashore, to the soft civilian life of the shore-side navy, and were exposed to all its forgotten motivations of status and rank and petty privilege, we felt ourselves to be apart. We felt ourselves to be older, wiser, and tougher than these spoilt and silly people, preoccupied with illusions. They seemed unaware of the harsh realities of the uncaring universe that enfolded their little make-believe society; a universe whose awesome power and certainty could be glimpsed in the moon-lonely wastes of the winter ocean.

Pride kept us at sea, month after month, year after year; to leave your ship and get a berth ashore was to yield, to surrender, to let the side down.

Pride was one factor; resentment was the other. Resentment of the shore-oriented organization of the Canadian

127

navy, which cast everyone in the little ships of the escort
fleet, officers and men, in the role of poor relations of their
counterparts in the big institutions ashore. Not only was promotion difficult for officers at sea, but for enlisted men as
well; ashore was where the courses were that led to higher ratings, higher rank, higher pay. It was commonplace for a ship
to leave a trouble-maker in prison cells ashore, only to return
a few months later and find that he had been made leading
hand, or even petty officer. He had been available ashore
when a course for the higher rating was beginning, while his
more competent shipmates had been far away at sea. This
was the case for officers also; if they were to advance or to
specialize, they had to come ashore. The first of our class
from RMC to reach the rank of lieutenant-commander was an
officer put ashore as incompetent from his only ship. He was
promptly put in charge of a shore training establishment and
raised in rank. An officer who did one trip with us was
landed in Newfoundland suffering from "nerves". When we
returned from our next trip we found him swanking about as
lieutenant-commander, and spinning salty dips to impression-
able nurses about his "experience at sea".

But envy and resentment of the greater opportunities
ashore were only part of the sense of alienation felt by men
in the seagoing navy; it was the attitudes of the shoreside establishment that particularly rankled. Being sent to sea was
viewed by the majority of officers and men ashore as a form
of punishment, or, at best, as a sort of purgatory which had
to be endured for the briefest possible period, as a necessary
prelude to more exalted rank or a more rewarding shoreside
appointment.

To corvette crews, Halifax, or more precisely HMCS *Stadacona*, universally known as "Slackers", was the embodiment
of the shoreside establishment; oh, how we hated to be sent
to Halifax!

The wartime city itself was a curious place. Because of its
long association with military service in general, and the navy
in particular, its inhabitants were indifferent to the thousands
of young men from every part of Canada who crowded its
old-fashioned streets. There was none of the warmth and interest of St. John's to be found in Halifax; a reaction under-
standable in view of the enormous number of servicemen
who had engulfed their city and taken over their meagre
amenities. It is characteristic that Halifax, renowned for its
port, should turn its back on the harbour which alone gives it

significance. Even today the waterfront is hidden from view, virtually unapproachable from the shore. No sweeping waterfront promenades link harbour with city, no great avenues roll down its hills to the seafront wharves. Instead one can approach the port only through mean little streets, twisting alleys, shabby yards, and dilapidated warehouses. Halifax does everything it can to disown its port origins, and to keep the crude seagoing types who berth there at a decent distance.

Personally, I liked the city, with its wealth of historic sites and pleasant places—the North West Arm and Point Pleasant, Citadel Hill and Grand Parade, St. Andrew's Gardens and old St. Paul's—but I knew that most of my shipmates detested the place, with its shabby wooden buildings, flush with the sidewalk, its run-down tramcars, its seedy cafés.

Yet it was not the city itself that made Halifax so universally detested, but rather the base; Slackers was a synonym for everything corvette crews loathed about the shoreside navy. There were, to begin with, those peculiarly precious officers who affected pseudo-British accents and aped the mannerisms of the Royal Navy, with Beatty buttons left undone and a handkerchief up the sleeve. I once overheard a pair of these exquisites in the dockyard canteen, languidly discussing their social round, shopping coups by their wives, and related matters. Eventually they discussed where they might forgather for drinks and dinner that evening; one of them proposed a well-known hotel.

"Oh, not that place," objected the other. "All those fellows off the ships go there!"

Halifax, in a word, was indifference; nobody seemed to care whether you lived or died. Base officers had a way of showing up on the jetties towards noon, to enjoy drinks and lunch aboard the ships before heading back to their offices. They accepted the hospitality of corvette wardrooms as no more than their due, and there were always remarks about "how lucky you fellows in the ships are to get all that cheap out-of-bond booze," but there was no suggestion that hospitality might be returned at their own mess ashore. Oh, ships' officers could lunch or dine at Admiralty House—most of us did—but at your own expense, of course; the fellow who'd drunk your gin and eaten your lunch aboard the day before would likely regard you with a fishy eye and have difficulty remembering your name if you approached him in his mess ashore. You could take in a movie at the regular *Stadacona* showings for base officers, and our matelots could use the *Stadacona* canteen, but always you were an outsider, an interloper in a creased uniform who hadn't seen last week's amusing picture at the Capitol and didn't know the price of drinks at the interval bar.

The one big drawing card for ship's officers in Halifax was the Saturday night dinner dance at the Nova Scotian Hotel, famed throughout the Western Approaches as "The Rat Race". Its principal attraction was that it made it possible for wardroom officers of each ship to go "on the town" in a body, which was the clannish custom in escort ships, so that ships of one group might have several adjoining tables. As a result, the Rat Race was a wonderful place for fellows just arriving in port to blow off steam, and the resultant high-jinks gave the Rat Race a raffish reputation still cherished to this day in the memories of middle-aged men. Everyone has his own particular recollection of incidents there; the one we recall that seemed most characteristic was the time the shore patrol made its appearance, caps neatly tucked under their elbows in deference to their surroundings, and made its way over to our ship's table. The petty officer in charge begged our pardon in respectful fashion, and then, before our astounded eyes, lifted the linen tablecloth and gently but firmly removed from beneath it the tousled officer who, all unbeknownst to us, had gone to ground there to escape the pursuing patrol after some run-in with authority. There was the night one high-spirited officer attempted to swing from a chandelier, reached by a shaky tower of tables and chairs. The chandelier, alas, proved to be a thing of straw, but apart from a little fallen plaster and broken glass, little harm was done, surely? In wartime Halifax, the Rat Race was where it was all at, and about the only happy event on the sombre Haligonian scene.

For men on the lower deck, Halifax was a virtual desert. Swarming ashore from crowded messdecks at the end of a long voyage, they found little to entertain them there, apart from the handful of crowded movies, seedy cafés, and the wet canteen. In later years there were games on the sportsgrounds ashore and film showings for the duty watch on board, organized by base sports and recreation officers, but Halifax, perhaps because of its size and the numbers of men cooped up in barracks and ships, never got around to providing the range of activites laid on for ships' crews in other ports, particularly Newfyjohn. Boredom in barracks and frustration in the messdecks of ships alongside bred a growing anger and tension in Halifax, a feeling intensified by the base's "9 to 5" and "long-weekend" mentality, which left the dockyard virtually deserted except for thousands of men cooped up in berthed ships. The shocking and disgraceful riots on VE day which tore Halifax apart sickened us, and most men in the escort ships by then based in Newfoundland or overseas, but for all of that they did not surprise us. Given the poor discipline and frustrations of Slackers, such an explosion was inevitable.

Women, or rather the lack of women, were a major problem which Canadian shore authority never faced up to. Nobody who has not experienced them can appreciate the frustrations bred in strong young men, in the prime of their youth, cooped up for weeks at a time under conditions that tried mind and body to the breaking point, without so much as the sound of a woman's voice, or the glimpse of a woman's face. Certainly, authority ashore seemed unable to comprehend the terrible need bred by such unnatural circumstances; to men living comfortable, well-balanced lives in normal society, the craving of Jack ashore for women was deplorable but rather amusing, an occasion for sly jokes and knowing winks.

European navies, older and wiser, provided brothels, carefully supervised and medically inspected, for men living under discipline and deprivation; the Americans provided dances and entertainment and thousands of pretty, respectable girls, for the sight and sound and touch of a woman can sublimate the basic urge. But in Halifax, the conventional morality of people living conventional lives could neither countenance a licensed brothel nor comprehend its need; and the means and will to provide alternatives such as was done by Mainguy with dances and other distractions in Newfyjohn seemed totally lacking.

The result was that whores, too old or diseased to earn a living on the pavements of other Canadian cities, hustled a brisk and profitable trade on the shabby streets of downtown Halifax, their white galoshes and their decrepitude becoming notorious throughout the Western Approaches. The resultant VD rate (the highest in any of the Allied services) took a greater toll of Canadian sailors than anything the Germans could do; venereal disease decimated the crews of Canadian ships. But the psychological damage wrought by guilt and fear and shame in youngsters deprived of normal healthy feminine company was equally damaging. Private enterprise hastened to fill the void left by official indifference; an enterprising businessman opened a discreet brothel in a big old house on Barrington Street, staffed it with a lot of pretty French-Canadian girls, and did so well that he opened a branch in Dartmouth. But from first to last, shore authorities seemed incapable of appreciating the intense frustrations imposed on thousands of young Canadians by an unnatural life under brutal conditions. The challenge was never met, the problem never faced; medication and punishment were the only responses.

In the ships, we could never understand why it was so difficult to get the essential supplies necessary to maintain efficiency, especially when enormous stocks were on hand. Paint, for instance. Paint keeps a steel vessel from disintegrating into a heap of rust, and in a small ship, constantly at sea in bad weather, painting is a never-ending task. Yet ships were never able to draw enough paint for their needs—even of the poor-quality paint that Canada provided for its navy. (British and American paint was much superior to anything available to us in Canada.) Vast stocks of paint were accumulated in stores ashore; what was it being saved for? How could a ship possibly use too much paint, when paint was esssential to maintain not only appearance, but the durability of the very fabric of the ship? It was the same with cordage, or shackles, or any other piece of equipment; a corvette the stock-keepers assured us, was not entitled to draw the item we wanted for our towing gear. What *were* they saving it for; a battleship? We were the only ships they had, we were the ones that had to tow ships at sea; why not give us the gear we needed?

Two pairs of Oerlikon guns, installed by the British aboard a corvette I was in to beef up our anti-aircraft defence, were taken away on return to Halifax because they were in excess of guns allotted to corvettes by authority. Nobody explained to us why the guns were more useful sitting in storage ashore than in action afloat.

As a result of this kind of negative thinking, corvette commanders were forced to revert to their own resources to fit out and equip their ship for efficiency. Scrounging parties were part of the answer; anything not actually nailed down was considered fair game by roving first lieutenants and bosuns. For a bottle of rum, a storekeeper could be persuaded to look the other way, and provided the operation was carried out with speed and dispatch a gang of husky seamen could come away with some surprising booty. When the liner *Rajputana* was being stripped out at Esquimalt early in the war for conversion to an armed merchant cruiser, hundreds of marvellous arm-chairs, mirrors, drapes, and other luxury furnishings were stacked on the jetty, en route to storage. From our corvette, fitting out across the jetty, we watched the mounting piles of goodies with drooling chops; the contrast to our own threadbare austerity was too much to bear.

Our moment came at the lunch-hour break; all the dockyard mateys trooped off to munch their sandwiches somewhere in the shade, and the instant the coast was clear half a hundred burly matelots were hard at work. Mirrors and electric fans for the messdecks, a fine pair of brocaded arm-chairs for the wardroom, and the pick of the lot, naturally, for the petty officers' mess: a great overstuffed settee.

The settee was too large to get down the hatch; like some monstrous caterpillar too large to get down an anthill hole, it stuck out of the fo'c'sle door while a dozen sweating figures toiled to squeeze it in. Within seconds the ship's carpenter took over, slit open the bottom, unbolted the legs, and slid the gorgeous carcass in and down the ladder, to be reassembled in all its glory within minutes. For the next two years our corvette was to be famous for the luxury of her fittings, and as the *Rajputana* was ultimately lost, she never returned for her missing furnishings.

Sometimes, of course, scrounging led to disaster; consider the sad case of Ted Briggs, the bearded bird who was later to head the CBC, and who was already renowned throughout the escort fleet for his unique gimballed table. The lively motion of his corvette *Orillia* had prompted Briggs to put in hand an experiment designed to make it easier to eat in bad weather, which made dining difficult because of the constantly tilting table. Since gimbals, or interlocking rings, permitted a compass to remain steady in bad weather, Briggs reasoned they ought to do the same for a table. Accordingly, he had the thing done; *Orillia* emerged from refit with the only gimballed table in the fleet, and in the first spot of bad weather, it was eagerly put to the test. Sure enough, the table remained level despite *Orillia*'s wildest leapings; what Briggs had not bargained for, however, was diners who were not in gimbals too. They went up and down with the ship, their chairs firmly on the deck, with the result that the table was at one moment at their knees, the next moment at their heads. Worse still; if one was caught with so much as an elbow over the table when the ship rolled, the swinging table promptly spilled its entire contents into one's lap. The gimballed table was relegated to an honoured place in the folklore of the corvette navy, and *Orillia*'s officers went back to dining in the lesser discomfort of a fixed table.

Briggs big moment arrived when he was patrolling off the Normandy beaches just after the invasion D-Day, as senior officer of a group of Canadian frigates. In the aftermath of the initial assault, an enormous amount of matériel was floated off the beaches, and the seas were littered with every conceivable item of military paraphernalia. Eagerly checking out this fascinating flotsam, Briggs spotted a DUKW, an amphibious truck which could chug along on both land and sea. The ideal vehicle, thought Briggs, for a seagoing senior officer; one could use it to go ashore from the ship, and then proceed on land as in a jeep. All hands were mustered, therefore, and while the other ships of the group patrolled around him in a protective ring, he attempted to get the thing aboard.

The trouble was, the vehicle weighed tons, and the frigate had no cargo boom, derrick, or davit capable of swaying such an object inboard. With consummate seamanship, however, Briggs rigged a tackle from his mast, giving him the necessary height, and led the tail to his windlass to be heaved in. As the tackle took the weight of the heavy truck, the ship began to heel sharply under the strain, the shrouds supporting the mast tightened bar taut, and everyone aboard held his breath. But not for long; just as the big vehicle started to lift upward from the water, there was a rending crash and overside went DUKW, tackle, shrouds, and the whole mainmast; the strain had snapped it off just a few feet above the level of the bridge. A chastened Briggs was forced to abandon the DUKW to the fortunes of the sea, and retire to port to lick his wounds and repair the damage.

Worse was to follow. The base commander, already up to his ears in repairs to invasion-damaged ships, was so furious at what he considered the frigate's self-inflicted wound that he refused to repair or replace the mast, and Briggs was forced to return to sea with only a stump, from which he constantly flew a single-flag signal. We encountered him in this condition, the group trailing disconsolately astern, and on looking up the meaning of his flag hoist found that it was: "Ships should closely observe movements of their leader, as

he may alter course and speed without further signal." The
sorry spectacle was a lesson to all of us, arrant scroungers to
a man.

What could not be obtained by official action or by
scrounging could sometimes be secured by bribery, with
bottles of rum as the medium of exchange. Almost every
worthwhile addition or alteration, which converted a corvette
from its basic Stone Age beginnings to the sophisticated
weapon it ultimately became, was brought about by ships' officers, at their own expense, bribing dockyard workmen to effect improvements which would not otherwise be made. So
many bottles for a "monkey island", or elevated con position;
so many more for wooden bridge dodgers instead of the canvas ones offically called for; for a compass platform here and
signal projectors there, for a ladder here and voice-pipes led
there. Little by little, the ship was made more habitable, more
efficient, more convenient, always at the expense and instiga-
tion of its own officers. No two corvettes were exactly alike
in bridge or accommodation layout. Voice-pipe location was
always a favourite subject for individual alteration to accommodate the particular needs of particular commanding officers. I can remember being intrigued by a voice-pipe fitted
in a bridge wing apparently to accommodate a midget, for its
bell-shaped copper mouth reached little more than knee-
height, only to learn that it led only overside, and had been
fitted as a urinal at the wish of a commanding officer who
virtually lived on the bridge while at sea.

Yet this official indifference to the needs and conditions of
individual men and ships in the escort fleet was probably
inevitable, given the inflated size and multiplying concerns of
naval authority. It was certainly accepted as such, and in
good heart, by corvette ships' companies. What was harder to
accept was the manning policy which prevailed in Canada,
and which prevented a ship ever sailing with the same complement twice in succession. In British escort ships, particularly in the later years of the war, serious—and
successful—efforts were made to retain officers and crew
aboard a ship for the length of its commission, or for the
year or so between refits. In this way a trained and disciplined team was built up, and the efficiency of a ship raised
as close as possible to perfection.

This was never possible in Canadian escorts, particularly in
ships working out of Halifax. As soon as a ship's officers and
men began to shape up as a team, experienced men would be

drafted off ashore. Each time a ship left harbour the process of training and indoctrination would have to begin again. This was to be the single greatest obstacle with which Canadian ships had to contend, and the biggest impediment to operational efficiency. No attempt was ever made in the RCN to concentrate the best-trained, best-qualified men at sea; instead, our finest experienced men and our most skillful specialists were to be found ashore, in training establishments or offices.

How we envied such crack groups as Britain's famed Second Escort Group, developed and trained by the redoubtable Johnny Walker! In these ships every position in the anti-submarine team was filled by the finest, best-qualified man available, a real galaxy of star performers. The formation of such an élite group of picked men was completely alien to Canadian naval authority; right to the war's end the practice of fobbing off problem officers and men from big shore bases to ships at sea, particularly those going overseas to another theatre of operation, was carried on. When I asked for a competent watch-keeping officer for a ship about to take part in the Normandy assault, Halifax authorities sent me the spoiled son of a Toronto millionaire, who'd been a disciplinary problem ashore, and who was afraid to go to sea. When he jumped ship before sailing; we were sent as replacement another problem child from barracks; this one proved to be not only incompetent and insubordinate, but a homosexual to boot.

Yet for all the differences between ship and shore, between "us and them", it was not until the closing months of the war that any real bitterness began to show itself in the ship's companies. In part the increasing sourness was due to the inevitable disillusionment and cynicism following a time of high emotional involvement. Our crusade, begun as a clear contest between freedom and tyranny, a picture painted in sharp black and white, was ending in a confused scene of drab greys. Tales coming back from Murmansk showed our Russian ally to be a tyrant at least as odious as the Nazis. Our own clear goal, to survive and keep freedom alive, had now long been swallowed up in squabbles about postwar spheres of influence. Even more upsetting from our point of view was the new wave of braggadocio, of boastful national assertiveness, inaugurated by public relations officers for the benefit of "the folks at home". This clashed violently with the traditional low profile, the almost obsessive understatement, of the Royal Navy, "The Silent Service", which we had absorbed, and which valued a modest demeanour above all else. We were first amused, then embarrassed, and eventually sickened, by the vainglorious accounts of the new breed of PR men, which exaggerated and distorted the role of Canadian servicemen and made us ridiculous in the eyes of Allies with whom we'd shared so much. (The first 1,000-bomber raid by Britain's RAF was headlined by our paper as "Halifax Man Bombs Berlin".) We all thought it uproariously funny when Vice-Admiral George C. Jones, a solid, unspectacular officer of vast seniority known to everyone as "Jetty Jones" (presumably because of all those peacetime years spent lying alongside), was given a "new image" by the PR people and launched in the media as Admiral George "Tiger" Jones! We did not think it so funny when we began to realize that we were being manipulated to accord with political purposes ashore, and that the public was accepting the ridiculously excessive accounts of media men at face value. Sourly, we refused to wear the gaudy shoulder flashes and meaningless service medal ribbons now being dished out, and we treasured still the civilian plainness of our sombre naval uniforms, which contrasted with the pomp and panache and boastfulness of the Americans that seemed to have infected our people ashore. Yet it remained for a couple of incidents overseas, in British ports, to deepen the growing cynicism and alienation of long-service men afloat into something like real anger.

In 1944 a large number of Canadian ships were based in Devonport for the Normandy build-up. When the commanding officers of these ships attempted to use the dockyard chapel for the funeral of half a dozen men killed aboard our *Haida* during a raiding action off the French coast, we were told by a plummy-voiced RN chaplain that only he could preside there; our own Canadian padre could not conduct a service within the sainted precincts. And, he added, only the Church of England man could be buried from there; we would have to take the others somewhere else.

This pedantic reaction was typical of the growing administrative obsession with form and forms which was blunting our fighting edge at sea. It did not seem to matter to those ashore just what you achieved at sea, so long as you filled in the correct returns ashore, and in quadruplicate, of course.

Our mounting resentment and confusion were heightened

by the inability of Canadian authorities to comprehend the conditions under which we were operating abroad. For months at a time, the ships of the two Canadian Normandy minesweeping flotillas were based at anchorages miles from the nearest shore facility. The motorboats we once carried had been removed in Canada and replaced with Carley floats. To get ashore, even for the most urgent business, we had to make a long pull in our whaler against strong tides, or rely on the hard-pressed boat services provided at long intervals by the port authority. Our grumbling was not improved by a signal received from some officious ass in Ottawa, who ordered us to land every curtain and tablecloth in the ship, because of a potential smoke hazard should the ship catch fire!

To tiny ships like ours, smoke from a burning curtain was the least of our concerns, but what rankled with us was not so much the stupidity of the signal as the incomprehension of its sender. Didn't he know that a ship was more than a weapon; that it was also our home? Didn't he know that to the more than one hundred men cooped up for months in this cramped metal box a bit of curtain, a cloth on the table, meant the difference between civilized standards and mere animal existence? Needless to say, we disregarded the signal in the finest Nelson tradition; but its dispatch, at a time when we were nerving ourselves to accept fifty-per-cent casualties in the coming assault on Fortress Europe, seemed indicative of the blindness to our realities of a shore authority obsessed with its own petty concerns.

In the hectic days following the first landings on the Normandy beaches, the British cable-ship *St. Margaret,* escorted by the Canadian corvette *Trentonian,* was laying a communication cable to the beach-head when they were attacked during the night by an American destroyer. The attack, of course, was inexcusable; the American commanding officer had failed to read the signal informing him that the cable-ship would be at work in his patrol area. But it was his persistence in the attack, once the identity of the cable-ship was clear, that was positively criminal. The destroyer lit up the civilian ship with star shell, then pounded the unarmed vessel with salvoes from close range, shifting fire to the Canadian corvette when she attempted to intervene. Eventually American bridge officers prevailed on their captain (a glory-hunter, they later explained to us) to cease fire. The American vessel then attempted to come alongside its shattered victim, but the fury of the British seamen, and of the Canadian corvette crew, prompted its crestfallen captain to make a prudent exit into the blackness of the night. The cable-ship was a shell-torn wreck, littered with badly wounded men; her captain died in the arms of Bill Harrison, *Trentonian*'s commanding officer. The shattered ships—*Trentonian* had a hole through her engine room—limped back to Portsmouth.

The American destroyer carried on unscathed. But when corvette and cable-ship made harbour, they were immediately isolated in a remote corner of the port, denied all liberty, and cut off from any communication with the shore. For some authority had become obsessed with the idea that if their story ever became known, it would create anti-American feeling in Britain and Canada, and accordingly the two inno-cent crews were imprisoned aboard their ships. After her Portsmouth exile ended, *Trentonian* was sent to sea. Shortly afterward she was torpedoed and sunk, thereby relieving shore authority of any further embarrassment.

The incident was soon common knowledge, and our fury at this monstrous injustice was deep and abiding. It was not directed so much at the U.S. captain—Americans were noto-riously trigger-happy and it was accepted as the other side of their aggressiveness—as at the ruthless and cynical manipula-tion of ships and men by our shore authority. It convinced us at last that it was not what happened that really mattered, so much as what you told the public had happened. We had learned the lessons taught by Goebbels, and now the pupil was besting the master.

With disbelief came disillusion; a growing cynicism soured our attitude to the whole vast image of Allied success. The enormous torrent of words, celebrating our glorious achieve-ments on land and sea and air, engendered only a mounting bitterness. Ironically, we found ourselves almost envying our old antagonists, the U-boat crews; they, at least, had been able to maintain their integrity and firmness of purpose, and had fought bravely to the end against hopeless odds. I can remember the real admiration we felt on visiting, after VE day, the surrendered U-boat that we had hunted, with no fewer than thirty-one other ships, right in the approaches to Plymouth, where it had just sunk a small fishing vessel. The guts of these German kids, shaken and shattered by bombing in port and depth-charging at sea, impressed us deeply; their demeanour robbed me of any savour in our triumph, now usurped and corrupted by boastful politicans, both service and civilian.

The little world, the private war, of the corvette navy was coming to an end, and all we wanted was out.

10
SIGNAL LOG

∿∿∿∿∿∿∿∿∿∿∿∿∿∿∿∿∿∿∿∿∿∿∿∿∿∿∿∿∿∿∿∿∿∿∿∿∿

The little coal-burning trawler, the smallest member of our escort as we shepherded our convoy off the Scottish coast, was investigating an under-water contact; the large flag attesting to this fact fluttered from her foremast. She was hardly moving as we watched her through the glasses, probing beneath the surface with her primitive asdic. Then her hoist went close-up to the yard-arm, indicating she was attacking with depth-charges. "My God, at that speed she'll blow herself out of the water," someone gasped on the bridge beside us. We watched in mingled horror and incredulity as suddenly the ocean all about the little ship erupted in towering fountains which blotted out all sight of her.

After what seemed an eternity, the little trawler came into view again—but what a change! Her stern staff had disappeared, blown clean off; she had a list to port and her steering gear had been damaged, so that she described a slow circle as she lost way through the water, finally coming to a stop with clouds of steam pouring from her engine-room skylight.

The spell which had gripped us was broken as her signal lamp began to chatter; we read the simple message as it spelled out: "I HAVE BUSTED MYSELF."

Signals like this, which capture a whole situation in a few terse words, are treasured by everyone who served in the escort ships, and everyone has his own particular favourite. Signals best embody the wit and humour of the navy, sometimes erudite and apt, sometimes coarse, but always pithy and to the point. After all, when each letter, word, or phrase has to be signalled by lamp or flag, one is at pains to be as brief as

possible, and the consequent sharpening of wit and style led
to some gems of bantering brevity.

What could be shorter, for example, than the greeting
flashed by the destroyer *Restigouche* ("Rustyguts" to her
friends, "Guts" to her group), whose pennant number was
HOO, to the little auxiliary vessel bearing the identifying number YOO:

From HOO to YOO: "YOO HOO."

In the interest of brevity, a number of senior officers of escort, particularly those from the RN, developed the habit of
sending signals to errant ships in the group which contained
merely a biblical reference of chapter and verse; the recipient
would have to have recourse to his Bible and, after looking
up the quotation, would "get the message". This business of
biblical signals became a great cult, so that it was necessary
to keep both a Bible and a concordance, which grouped
references under various classifications, handy on the bridge
at sea. We received a typical example of such a message one
night when we had inadvertently strayed out of station. As
we scrambled shamefacedly back into station in broad daylight our senior officer blinked a biblical reference to us
which, on being checked out, gave us: "MY GOD, MY GOD,
WHY HAST THOU FORSAKEN ME."

Almost every situation, every nuance of meaning, could be
found in the vast reaches of the Bible. A treasured example
was the signal sent by Commander-in-Chief, Plymouth, to a
corvette towing a damaged merchantman:

From corvette to C. in-C. Plymouth: "ROMAN EMPEROR IN
TOW, BADLY DAMAGED, PLEASE SEND TUGS."

From C. in-C. Plymouth: "REVELATIONS CHAPTER 3 VERSE
11." ("Behold, I come quickly; hold that fast which thou
hast, that no man take thy crown.")

Then there was the classic which went the rounds of the
wardrooms: the signal sent by a commanding officer in response to a message of congratulations upon his receiving
promotion to lieutenant-commander. "VMT. PSALM 140, 2ND
HALF OF VERSE 5." ("Very many thanks. They have set gins
for me.")

The destroyer *Skeena*, seeking assistance to check out a
poor asdic echo which yet seemed suspiciously like that of a
submarine, sent a signal to the corvette *Wetaskiwin* which
touched off a famous hunt. The signal was simply: "ACTS 16,
VERSE 9." ("And a vision appeared to Paul in the night;

There stood a man of Macedonia and prayed him, saying, Come over into Macedonia and help us.")

Eager for the fray, *Wetaskiwin* came pelting over the horizon, sending as acknowledgement the brief signal: "REVELATIONS 13, VERSE 1." It was *Skeena*'s turn to thumb furiously through the pages of the bridge Bible, to turn up the reference "And I stood upon the sand of the sea, and saw a beast rise up out of the sea, having seven heads and ten horns, and upon his horns ten crowns, and upon his heads the name of blasphemy."

Not so apt and precise as some of the best of the biblical signals, perhaps, but considering it was done in the heat of the hunt, a hunt which was to result in the destruction of U588, it was pretty quick work, and raised a smile in many an escort yardroom and messdeck.

Some of the most savoured signals were at the expense of ships' names, of which there was an endless variety. Ships named for ladies were a favourite source of funny signals, including these gems from escorts: "GRACIE FIELDS MAKING WATER, OUT OF CONTROL," and "LOUISE EJECTED FROM CONVOY FOR EXCESSIVE SMOKING."

There was a good deal of archness in signals about Wrens. The first and most famous signal was said to have been sent with no double meaning intended in 1940. There were serious shortages of cloth at that time, resulting in conflicts between various branches of the service for the limited supply of material for uniforms. Indignant that his sailors were still in civilian clothes while girls entering the service were drawing uniforms without hindrance, an irate admiral made the following signal: "WRENS CLOTHING IS TO BE HELD UP UNTIL THE NEEDS OF SEAGOING PERSONNEL HAVE BEEN SATISFIED."

In Portsmouth, however, a reverse condition prevailed: uniforms for Wrens were in such short supply that over a thousand servicewomen were still in plain clothes. The C.-in-C. Portsmouth complained by signal: "AT SOME ESTABLISHMENTS NEW ENTRY WRENS ARE NOW WORKING IN BARE LEGS TO SAVE THEIR PAIR OF STOCKINGS FOR WALKING OUT. IN DUE COURSE A LARGE NUMBER OF WRENS WILL BE WORKING IN A STATE OF NATURE WHICH ON MANY GROUNDS WOULD BE UNDESIRABLE."

The sly response came from C.-in-C. Plymouth. "SUGGEST YOU APPLY FOR FIGHTER COVER."

References to women, of course, provided a constant source of humour in a force starved for their company. Everyone recalls the joyous disbelief of the escort returning to base on receiving the signal: "HAVE WOMEN FOR YOU." Inevitably, of course, a correction followed: "HAVE TWO MEN FOR YOU."

Perhaps the most famous signal of this sort was sent on the occasion of a squadron's arrival at an overseas station:

From Flag Officer to Senior Officer, Port: "WHO DO YOU RECOMMEND FOR ADMIRAL'S WOMAN."

The recipient of this signal, naturally dumbfounded, asked for a repeat of the message, and received the following amendment: "REFERENCE MY SIGNAL, PLEASE INSERT WASHER BETWEEN ADMIRAL AND WOMAN."

To corvette crews, of course, signals from shore authority sometimes seemed out of touch with the realities of the situation, and a particularly obtuse example was something to be treasured. But there were few that could match a famous exchange between the Admiralty and a destroyer in the earliest days of the war:

From Admiralty to destroyer: "PROCEED WITH ALL DESPATCH."

From destroyer to Admiralty: "REQUEST DESTINATION."

From Admiralty to destroyer: "ADEN, REPEAT, ADEN."

From destroyer to Admiralty: "AM AT ADEN."

Another classic was the interchange between a corvette, inward bound from sea, which had been damaged by a mine and had reported her conditions to shore authority as she limped into Liverpool. Feeling very much the battered warrior, home from the wars, bloodied but unbowed, and secretly wondering if they might not even be cheered into harbour by crews of ships alongside, the corvette crew were considerably miffed to receive, as the only acknowledgement of their suffering, the following terse signal from an unfeeling authority as they passed the Bar light vessel: "DO NOT SINK IN SWEPT CHANNEL."

In Canadian groups, a kind of cult would grow up around the style of signals between ships in the group. In some groups, for instance, the jargon of Damon Runyon, whose Broadway argot and guys and dolls were then very popular, was often used, and individual officers were known to one and all by Runyon nicknames: Harry the Horse, Good Time Charlie, etc. Other groups would use an affected British style for inter-ship signals, à la Bertie Wooster and Jeeves, while in other signals would be couched in a sort of burlesque Jewish style.

A couple of Canadian escorts were making their way into an East Coast anchorage blocked by pack ice; the first ship, forcing a passage, anchored inside and sent the following signal to her consort outside:

First ship to second: "ABIE, ABIE, ABIE, MINE BOY, WHAT ARE YOU WAITING FOR NOW."

Reply from second ship: "ICEHOLES."

Then there was the signal from one Canadian escort over-hauling another, racing for port: "DON'T LOOK NOW, BUT YOUR SHIP IS SLOWING."

Canadian reservists were notoriously impatient of the serv-ice nomenclature used in the Royal Navy, and hallowed by centuries of use; they would talk of "rowing" a boat, for in-stance, instead of the proper "pulling". The following signal is typical of such reproofs:

Canadian corvette to base: "AM TIED UP AT NO. 5 BERTH."

From base to corvette: "SHOE LACES ARE TIED UP. HM. SHIPS ARE SECURED."

A host of signals made in response to fussy authority were cherished by ships where "respectful irreverence" was a sort of art. One such pearl was the response of a corvette on being asked by an impatient base authority how long he would be before leaving harbour:

From corvette to base: "TWO HUNDRED AND FIVE FEET AS USUAL."

Or the one which, after making a botch of a mid-ocean manoeuvre, was asked by an irritable senior officer: "WHAT ARE YOU DOING."

Reply from corvette: "LEARNING A LOT."

Then there was the annoyed senior officer attempting to scold the corvette which was rejoining after a hunt astern in very bad weather.

Senior officer to corvette: "WHY HAVE YOU TAKEN SO LONG TO REJOIN CONVOY."

Corvette to senior officer: "IT WAS UPHILL ALL THE WAY."

And then:

From Port Authority to corvette: "WHAT IS ALL THAT LAUNDRY HANGING UP FOR."

Reply from corvette: "SUBMIT, TO DRY."

Signals to other branches of the service could sometimes be fun. Coming in to Portsmouth one evening, we signalled a very warlike-looking MTB growling out on patrol: "GOOD LUCK."

We received the saucy reply: "THANKS. ACTUALLY WE RELY ON SKILL."

And then of course, there was the air force. Towing a drogue for target practice by anti-aircraft gunners in the fleet was always a hairy business at best. Once, when a shell burst in front of the towing aircraft instead of near the target towed far astern, the indignant pilot made the classic protest: "I AM PULLING THIS BLOODY THING, NOT PUSHING IT."

Sometimes, too, the point of naval jokes was missed in the air, or vice-versa. The following interchange took place early in the war, with a ship encountering a coastal command aircraft off Rockall:

From aircraft: "WHAT SHIP."

From ship: "GRAF SPEE."

From aircraft: "ARE YOU NAVAL TYPES STILL SO FAST ASLEEP THAT YOU HAVEN'T HEARD OF THE END OF THE GRAF SPEE."

From ship: "WHICH END."

The besetting worry of ships at sea concerning their position produced many memorable signals, typical of which is the one signalled from one ship to another: "WHAT DO YOU MAKE OUR POSITION, OTHER THAN PRECARIOUS."

Off Omaha beach-head on the morning of June 6, 1944, a single landing-craft, loaded with troops, led an enormous armada, stretching back over the horizon as far as the eye could see, towards the beach ahead. She had been brought to precisely that position by all the marvels of modern science and good staff work; her route was marked by lighted buoys and lit up as brightly as Yonge Street on a Saturday night, her path swept and marked by ships with the most precise electronic navigational gear, and directly ahead a midget submarine lay on the surface transmitting a beam, by light and wireless, on which she could steer. Her arrival, in the vanguard of the greatest naval force ever seen, was both a technological triumph and an historic moment. As she moved past us, where we lay recovering our minesweeping gear off the beach, her signal lamp began to flash; some stirring, inspirational war-cry, perhaps, at this moment of ultimate confrontation?

Signal from landing-craft: "WHERE AM I."

And then there were the private signals. With thousands of homesick seamen writing home, anxious to convey intimate messages to loved ones without incurring the censor's attention, an ingenious system of communication was incorporated into letters to family, and especially to wives and girl friends. Postscripts were the most popular method, beginning with simple o's and x's scrawled at the bottom of a letter.

Censoring mail aboard ship was a thankless task, traditionally assigned to the most junior officer in the wardroom; it was his job to delete from all letters any mention of ship movements or military operations which could conceivably be of use to the enemy. As the war went on, censoring officers noted a growing trend to enigmatic postscripts, usually merely a few capital letters at the bottom of a page, or on the envelope itself. The cracking of these codes was perhaps the sole redeeming pleasure which censor officers derived from wading through dozens of letters home from lonely sailors, and even today the recollection of some of those messages can raise a smile. There was a simple H and K— Hugs and Kisses, and the equally ubiquitous SWALK—Sealed With A Loving Kiss. But a great cult developed later in the war, the so-called WICH message, introduced by RN ratings writing home to their wives. These posed a real challenge to censor officers, and ran the full gamut of the erotic imagination. Everyone's favourite was in the best tradition of the earthy society which had evolved the comic seaside postcard. It was NORWICH— (k) Nickers Off Ready When I Come Home.

Memory's logbook retains mostly the light, the frivolous, messages, sent from ship to ship; the great moments, the signals that initiated historic events, are mostly forgotten. The best signals were passed on as anecdotes, so that the ships actually involved tended to be forgotten and only their cheeky banter survives:

From ship to ship: "PLEASE SEND YOUR ARTIFICER TO SEE OUR FORWARD GUN."

Reply: "OUR ARTIFICER CAN SEE YOUR FORWARD GUN FROM HERE."

From senior officer, whose ship has just been run into, to his crestfallen assailant, now backing off: "WHAT DO YOU INTEND TO DO NOW."

Reply: "BUY A FARM."

Two escorts approaching Portland in thick fog, visibility nil:

First escort: "WHEN DO YOU EXPECT TO SIGHT PORTLAND BREAKWATER."

Reply: "FIFTEEN MINUTES AGO. ESTIMATE MY POSITION FOURTH FAIRWAY GOLF COURSE."

And then, of course, there is the marvellous old turkey about the new ship berthing for the first time under the approving eye of the port admiral. The ship made a good approach to an awkward berth, and appeared to have judged matters to a nicety, so the admiral signalled, approvingly: "GOOD."

But then everything went wrong; a breastline parted, and the new arrival ground along the bows of the ship astern. A horrified admiral made another signal: "ADD TO MY PREVIOUS SIGNAL, GOD."

Aircraft carriers of all sizes were ungainly ships, a favourite target for insulting banter. When a fleet carrier appeared from refit, gleaming in fresh paint, she signalled a passing escort:

From carrier: "HOW DO I LOOK."

Reply from escort: "GO BACK TO LOCH NESS."

A Canadian escort carrier, disabled at sea and entering harbour under tow, took an awkward sheer and set down upon the gate vessel as she passed through the boom defence, doing considerable damage to the little vessel's paintwork. Weeks later, after the carrier had been repaired and headed down harbour for sea, a waggish corvette lying near by signalled to the boom-defence gate vessel: "LOOK OUT, HERE SHE COMES AGAIN."

A senior officer escort, dispatching a damaged corvette to base for repairs, sent her on her way with a fond wish:

S.O. to corvette: "HOPE YOU FIND FACILITIES YOU NEED IN BELFAST."

Despondent corvette to S.O.: "HOPE I FIND BELFAST."

But of all the signals ever made by ships of the escort navy, surely one of the last was one of the best; certainly the best-remembered, and in its cheekiness and brevity, typical of the wartime corvette navy. Newfoundland in signal jargon was N.F.; the flag officer in command of the base was Flag Officer, Newfoundland, or F.O.N.F.

At the war's end, a corvette leaving Newfoundland for home made the following famous signal:

From corvette to F.O.N.F.: "REQUEST PERMISSION TO F.O. FROM N.F."

11
THE CHANNEL WAR

In the spring of 1944, a wonderful thing happened to a lot of us in Western Approaches; after years of bashing into North Atlantic gales, we transferred operations to the English Channel and its approaches from the Bay of Biscay and the Irish Sea. In preparation for the coming cross-Channel invasion, Canadian frigates and corvettes set up patrol lines at the western entrance of the Channel to deny the assault area to any U-boat intrusion, or reinforced the escort of the vital strategic-cargo convoys now entering British ports. But for those of us in steam Bangors, the change was even more welcome; after weary years of escort, these fine twin-screw little ships were to be fitted out for the fast minesweeping duties they were designed for, and sent across to lead the way through the minefields and on into the invasion beaches. Our quarterdecks heavy with new floats and sweeps, and bristling with new high-angle three-inch guns forward and power-operated twin Oerlikons aft, we felt capable of taking on the Luftwaffe single-handed; in the event, we were not called upon to do so.

It would be difficult to conceive a more dramatic change in circumstances than the transfer to the Channel from the North Atlantic. Gone were the frightful winter weather, the incessant gales, the long, wearying hauls across the endless reaches of featureless ocean. Suddenly, things got much more civilized; distances were shorter, passages faster, the weather better; always there was a choice of ports under your lee in case of trouble. Reinforcements were only hours, sometimes even minutes away. By getting on the blower, you could whistle up air cover or call over a couple of support groups to bear a hand, while tugs and pumps were always available in case of collision or torpedoing. Ships could make port with damage that would have meant certain loss in the vast Atlantic; fuelling became a mere harbour function, and we could complete a whole trip without running out of bread.

Equally intriguing was the nearness and variety of the enemy menace. You had to be concerned about him, even in harbour; he could bomb you there or strafe you in the Channel, or blow you up with the guided glider-bomb, Hitler's latest. There were doodle-bugs in season, along with E-boats, fast, and R-boats, slow; Elbing (small) and Narvik (big) destroyers, flak ships, U-boats, and miniature submarines; mines (moored), mines (pressure), mines (acoustic), mines (magnetic), mines (electric), mines (controlled), mines (contact), mines (theirs), and mines (ours); most surprising and most dangerous of all, there were the heaviest and most accurate and most belligerent shore batteries imaginable.

After the dreary, boring months of shepherding convoys across the briny, the variety and proximity of the enemy was most stimulating; you could leave harbour, have a rousing punch-up with Adolf's lot in one form or another, and be back in harbour without missing a meal. Navigationally, too, it was a whole new ball game; gone were the noonday observations and star-shots. Now we were back into doubling angles on the bow and running fixes, for not only land but usually a prominent lighthouse or two was in sight. We stowed our sextants away and quickly became familiar with the characteristics of a new set of landmarks, set out like lamp-posts along a busy street; the Wolf and Bishop, Longships and the Lizard, the Eddystone and Start, Portland and Beachy Head.

And oh, the change in weather. It could get nasty in the Channel, of course, with lots of wind and steep seas and bad visibility, but the Channel chop was a world away from those giant Atlantic combers, and the radar we had nowadays removed many of the terrors of fog in convoy, although the great volume of traffic through the Channel and the close quarters could make things a bit dodgy on a thick night.

Everyone welcomed the change, and for those of us lucky enough to be in a Bangor, these were great days. At sea we applied ourselves to mastering the techniques of a new kind of warfare, with its emphasis on tight formation and meticulous station-keeping; ashore we revelled in the infinite variety England—even war-weary, austere, England—offered its visitors. For although our leave was limited to a few hours in port or a run to London during a boiler-clean, a marvellous train and bus system seemed able to transport us almost anywhere in the country in a matter of a few hours. For Canadians accustomed to a train a day in either direction at home, the frequency of British trains was a revelation; you could catch a train to London from Portsmouth about every twenty minutes!

It was an exciting place to be, at an exciting time. The country was a vast armed camp, full of the soldiery of all the free World, and full, too, of an air of exultation. For everyone knew that we were on the brink of a great adventure, an assault, on a scale never seen before in all the world, on the bastions of Nazi Europe. For long, weary years Britain had been battered and beleaguered by the armed might of oppression; now the forces of freedom, from all over the world, had rallied to this war-worn island, and Britain and the British reflected a new and confident mood.

London was the centre of the world in those great days, or so it seemed to us on our brief visits there on leave. Gielgud was in *Hamlet* at the Haymarket, Ivor Novello's *Perchance to Dream* was playing to packed houses, Richard Tauber was filling a battered London theatre with lovely Strauss waltzes and arias from *Gay Rosalinda*, and if you were lucky, you could get to see George Robey or Max Miller and hear the bluest, funniest jokes imaginable. Those stunning girls were still posing in nude tableaux at the Windmill, and some of the finest musicians in all the world were playing every noon-hour at the National Gallery before milling masses of uniforms.

And, of course, all those thousands of servicemen had presented the Piccadilly Commandos with their greatest challenge; they hurried, as fast as they could on their high heels, from their beat in the Circus to their shabby rooms in some bomb-battered building near by to keep up with the demand. "I'll give you ever such a good time, ducks, but just a short time only, mind," It was their finest hour.

But London for us was for the infrequent "boiler-clean" leaves; mostly our time was spent in the rural loveliness of Devon and Cornwall, for we were based out of Plymouth. On an afternoon off, we could nip ashore, into the yawning emptiness of the city centre (for the whole middle of the place, miles of it, had been completely gutted by fire-bombs early in the war), and catch a bus to anywhere, our destination just a

name on the bus front. We were never disappointed; we discovered Fowey and Looe and St. Ives, Dartmoor and Cock-
ington and Buckfast Abbey—all those incredibly beautiful
little ports and towns, set in the loveliest countryside we had
ever seen.

Meanwhile, we were making our flotilla, the 31st, the finest
minesweeping group in the Allied navies—or so we thought,
at any rate. Our own ship, *Minas*, we rated as best in our
flotilla; we could get our gear out or in faster than anyone,
and our signalling was sharper and our station-keeping more
rigid—or so, at least, it seemed to us, impartial judges to a
man.

We were conducting our exercises principally in Tor Bay, a
fine, sheltered anchorage, in anything except an east wind, on
the south Devon coast, a traditional bolt-hole for British
Channel fleets in westerly gales during the French wars. We
were supposed to anchor out there each night, or around the
corner in Babbacombe Bay, and so we did—at first.

But across the bay from us lay Torquay, with all the flesh-
pots of England's finest coastal resort. Its inner harbour dried
out at low water and its outer harbour was intended only for
yachts and small fishermen, but close examination of the
chart showed that there was just sufficient water alongside the
inner wall of the mole to float a Bangor at all states of the
tide, although it quickly shallowed a few yards out toward
the centre of the basin. Once we had discovered that, the die
was cast; for expert ship-handlers, as we had become, and
with twin-screw, handy ships, the thing was a piece of cake.
We would approach the end of the mole, one at a time, get a
line on the end bollard as a spring, and pivot ourselves
around the end of the mole and alongside just as slick as you
please, and we nested up alongside, two abreast; the biggest
ships, the locals told us, ever to berth inside.

At the end of the pier, immediately opposite, was a superb
theatre; five minutes after berthing we were all inside,
watching George Bernard Shaw explain the dilemma of *Mrs.
Warren's Profession*.

Those exercises were a great time for us. All day, in the
endless Devon sunshine, we steamed back and forth across
the blue waters of the bay, steaming and recovering gear, laying marker dan buoys, practising precise station-keeping. At
night, pleasantly weary, we would repair to the diversions of
Torquay, a base we had all to ourselves.

All good things come to an end. Adjudged fit and battle-worthy, we were shifted east to Portsmouth, henceforth our base, and already filled with the shipping readied for the great assault. Here, with vast numbers of other warships, landing craft, aircraft, and thousands upon thousands of soldiers, we engaged in a number of joint exercises in which a large number of men were actually landed on a shelving beach. It all culminated in the vast dress rehearsal (Exercise Trousers) off Chesil Beach, a long stretch of shingle stretching for miles westward from Portland Bill.

It was a schemozzle from start to finish; thick fog came down as the landing-craft, loaded with eager young soldiers, began their run in to the beach. Some of the craft grounded on an outer bar; the fog prevented them from seeing that they had not yet reached the true beach, and they lowered their ramps, disgorging their men into ten feet of water. Hundreds drowned. Adding to the confusion was a German R-boat, with an escort of faster E-boats, quietly laying mines off the beach. Caught by this vast armada looming out of the fog, they took off at a great rate of knots, racing past long columns of landing-craft whose soldiers looked blankly out at them as just another realistic touch to the exercise. It was difficult to say who was the more startled; we stared at the Germans haring past us, and they stared back at us, all of us "filled with a wild surmise". They disappeared into the night, pursued by the corvette *Mimico,* whose commander was henceforth to be known to all his friends as E-boat Elmsley.

"Trousers" was a frightful mess; we atoned for it with "Fabius", the final exercise, and a full-scale one, when we put thousands of men ashore near Selsey Bill, with everything going like clockwork. We were ready for the big one.

On the first of June we moved to our assault anchorage off Poole; all about us lay a vast assemblage of shipping of every kind, including such exotica as the Dutch gunboats *Flores* and *Soemba,* tiny vessels carrying a pair of enormous six-inch guns, and crewed by the blackest Negroes we had ever seen. All the great battleships of the bombarding force—*Warspite, Rodney, Valiant, Texas,* etc.—were there, along with all kinds of magnificent cruisers; the French *Gloire,* which we selected as the most beautiful warship we had ever seen, *Black Prince, Bellona,* and innumerable others. All the endless ramifications of specialist assault ships were there too; the rocket ships, their whole deck covered with hundreds of spigots on which rockets were fixed and fired; gun ships, flak ships, even cook ships, which carried galley facilities to service the innumerable small craft off the beaches.

The Germans sent aircraft over to bomb and strafe this enormous fleet, and the flak in the night sky from our concentrated gunfire was something to behold. The dark sky was filled with every sort of flak, orange, green, red, white; lines of tracer reached upward, bursts of bright luminescence floated high above, bright searchlight beams probed the high cloud cover above. It was an amazing sight, and it brought results; our twin Oerlikons shared honours with a Hunt-class destroyer in bringing down a Heinkel III which crashed right in the town after weaving low over the water.

The next day we, like everyone else taking part, were sealed off from any contact with the shore, and received our orders. Our flotilla was to lead the parade in to Omaha beach in the American sector, cutting a path through the minefields towards the little town of Port en Bessin, where we would sweep out an area in which the bombardment ships could do their stuff. Hopefully, we would then withdraw to let the first wave go past us, but since we would have been fooling around, at slow speed, a mile off the beach and in point-blank range of three big coastal batteries, we did not really expect to survive as a flotilla. In fact, we were told to expect thirty per cent to fifty per cent casualties, and we were provided with spare vessels ready to fill in the formation as required, a rather nice touch, we felt.

Operation Neptune, as the sea-borne assault at Normandy was called, was a miracle of staff work; nobody who saw it will ever forget the incredibly complex and complete volume of instructions and detailed descriptions furnished to each ship in the great attack. Everything was there, including a mosaic of photographs, from air and sea, of the entire coast-line of the Bay of the Seine; every tiny landmark, down to individual trees, was clearly indicated. Men had been working for years, from canoes and submarines and aircraft, to gather this information. The depths of water, the obstacles—and they were formidable—even the composition of the bottom, had been learned and indicated; the guidebook to Neptune was a triumph of organization carried to the level of art, of genius.

D-Day was set for June 5, and we would sail in the dark hours of early morning of the fourth in order to reach our rendezvous on time. I cleared lower decks when we had our orders and had a chat with all our people; we would have liked to be taking in our own Canadian troops, but we were enormously proud to be in the forefront of this tremendous affair, and felt it to be a fitting reward for all the endless years of convoy work in the North Atlantic. We made our wills, wrote our last letters home.

It blew hard that night, we weighed at 0245 and headed down channel from our new anchorage off Ryde in the Solent, and as we neared Horsesand fort it was blowing half a gale, with driving sheets of rain. A terrible night for an invasion, and the congestion of traffic, of every ship, great and small, all bound outward round Bembridge Point, was like Number 11 highway south from Lake Simcoe on a summer Sunday night. At six in the morning, just before we were committed to the sweep across, we were recalled; the invasion had been postponed for twenty-four hours, which cost our chief engineer the eight pounds he had won in the ship's D-Day pool, and gave us a wet day at anchor in the Solent.

Our little dan-layer, the former fish-drifter *Gunner,* missed the recall signal; her captain thought it odd that he somehow emerged from the heavy traffic all alone in the world, but he kept on in the driving rain, hoping to catch up the flotilla he was convinced had sailed ahead of him. He arrived off the appointed beach on the Normandy coast, found nobody, so anchored to await the march of events. He sat there, untouched, all that long day, under some of the most powerful guns in Europe; next day, when we arrived, he weighed and took station astern, wondering what had kept us.

The sweep across for us, once we had got clear of the incredible traffic jam east and south of the Isle of Wight, was simple enough. We got our sweeps at 5:30 in the afternoon, and two hours later we entered the enemy minefields, my knees shaking with patriotism as I kept close watch on *Cowichan* ahead for any mines she should cut. By midnight the show was on; the air force began to kick the stuffing out of the coast, and Port en Bessin ahead was a tremendous spectacle, with fires raging below and a fireworks show of flak and searchlights up above.

At three in the morning we did our thing, a slow turn to starboard, with the ship almost stopped, and so close to the beach we could make out every detail in the pale light of a wan moon. When we finished our turn, without a glove laid on us, we knew we were home free; from here on it was downhill all the way, a piece of cake. Behind us stretched a great wide channel of swept water, lit up by lighted dan buoys at regular intervals; off to starboard were two other similar channels, like lighted streets leading to the beaches, cut by "the famous Fourth", a fine old bunch of First World War coal-burners, and the 14th, a flotilla of mixed British and Canadian ships. The roads well and duly cut and blazed, we stood to one side, as the Coxswain said, "to watch the Pongoes get on with the job."

It was full daylight as we recovered our sweeps, right off the beach. To seaward was an unbelievable sight; every ship in the world seemed to be steaming over the horizon, heading for the beaches, now lying veiled under clouds of smoke from the night's bombing. Troop-carrying liners were headed for their anchorages, to off-load their men into assault boats; long lines of landing craft, infantry, and landing craft, tanks, were trundling along in close formation, while the big battleships and cruisers of the bombarding squadrons were taking up position and spitting in their palms, getting ready to buckle down to work.

For a moment we in the sweepers were conscious of an instant of almost heart-stopping intensity; a moment of historical confrontation between what seemed to us to be the forces of freedom and tyranny, of good and evil. Behind us to seaward all was light, the pale flush of dawn on the light paintwork, the bright white ensigns of the ships; ashore all was dark and sombre and sullen, the squat grey concrete of the German batteries, with their black slits and deep embrasures, like so many malformed skulls. For a long moment, we freemen looked for the first time on the dark forces we had fought against for so long, brought to bay at last like some fearful monster of romance; and they, in their bunkers and casemates ashore, surely they looked out at us, and saw at last their doom.

And then, sharp at ten minutes past five, our bombarding ships opened fire, and the fur began to fly. A French cruiser, the *Georges Leygues* ("George's Legs" to one and all), out of position and, as one would expect, in a panic to be somewhere else, nearly ran us down, but we went hard over and cut under his stern, unscathed save for a change of drawers all round. With our battle ensigns snapping in the breeze, we were getting our sweeps inboard, surrounded by assault boats of engineers going after the underwater obstacles in the shallows, when the first salvoes from the shore batteries arrived in our midst, speeding things up considerably among the toilers on the quarterdeck. *Blairmore*, next ship to us, was near-missed, a fountain of water towering up over her quarterdeck, and as she turned she was near-missed again, the water blowing right across her. The noise now was indescribable, with the reverberation of our own heavy guns as a constant thunderous rumble, orchestrated by lighter guns and bombs and bursting shells. Fleets of aircraft filled the air, both bombers and strings of troop-carrying gliders, headed inland; so intense was the racket that we could not hear ourselves speak. *Blairmore*'s mascot, a little white woolly dog and a great favourite, caught up in a world gone mad, went mad, too. He shot at high speed around the quarterdeck, then leaped over the side, never to be seen again; but despite the shells now falling in our midst, he was our flotilla's only casualty.

As we drew out to begin our next task, the headquarters ship *Largs* was flying the hoist "DRIVE ON!" It seemed as good a battlecry as any. Our wardroom steward, best in the navy, brought us breakfast on a tray; I breakfasted on the bridge, with a fresh linen napkin, in almost eighteenth-century elegance, amid all the noise and smoke of furious battle.

This day, and the week that followed, was the most exciting period of my life, so crammed with incident, so filled with tension and toil and exultation and excitement, that time quite lost its meaning. We worked from daybreak to darkness, sweeping the heavy minefields which shielded most of the coast. Mines were thick here; we cut them with the serrated wire of our sweep and with the steel cutter jaws at its end, then sank the floating mines with anti-tank rifles as they bobbed to the surface. Occasionally a round from the gun would hit a horn, and the mine would explode with a bang that would make us all pull long faces, as we thought what they could do to a little ship like ours. Once, manoeuvring to go alongside a tanker, the wash from our propellers touched off an oyster mine, and it went off just ahead of our bows, drenching us in a fountain of water but otherwise doing no damage. All about us the battle swirled and surged; we parted a sweep wire on the old U.S. battleship *Texas*, and had to recover it right under her turrets, the blast from her gun breaking our bridge windows as she pounded the beaches. For our lot had trouble ashore, the only beach that had; Omaha beach commander had fouled things up a bit by off-loading his men so far offshore that by the time they hit the beach the impact of the bombardment had passed, and the Germans were back at their guns and ready. To make things worse, the same commander had disdained the close fire support given the other beaches by amphibious tanks and other ingenious improvisations designed to wipe out the pill-box fire. As a result, his fellows got stuck on beaches domi-nated by steep cliffs, the most formidable geography of the whole area, and only by sending destroyers and gunboats right into the shallows—one destroyer we saw was so close they were using machine guns to fire at individual Germans running along the beach—and concentrating the fire of the big battleships on the cliff-tops was the assault finally able to get moving again.

The battleships, wreathed in smoke and flame, were stirring sights as we ploughed along past them, clearing mines so that they could move in a bit closer.

We lived intensely, in a chaotic, exciting milieu, and mostly on our nerves; we made the most of each precious hour of daylight and slept on briefly, for even at anchor each night the Germans sent marauding aircraft in under our fighter cover to bomb and strafe just off the beaches. It was exhausting, but after the long hours of shepherding convoys across the Atlantic it seemed wonderful to us.

And through it all, like a kind of theme, ran "Lili Mar-lene". The Allied Forces radio seemed to play nothing else; on the popular Mailbag show a dozen different renditions, with a dozen different singers, gave us Lili's haunting ballad. But the German rendition, with husky-voiced Lale Andersen, a bass chorus, and all those marching feet in the background, was by far the best. The Germans played it incessantly, and so did we; it had been the song of the desert armies, and now it became the melody of the invasion.

More than any other music, it captured the home-sick sen timentality of everyone who was far from home and his girl: "your sweet face seems, / to haunt my dreams." More to the point, there was a kind of fatalism, a sense of despair, that appealed to men caught up in great events. For whatever rea-son, Lale sang her song to all of us, hourly it seemed, and turned the imagination to your girl and to your dreams that could never come true, a passing relief from the demands and pressures of the present.

Every day brought its adventures. There was the midget submarine or "chariot" torpedo attack on ships at anchor off the beach, when a sailor looking idly over the side found himself staring at a man in the sea beneath him, in a sort of plastic bubble. There were the innumerable aircraft incidents, usually tragic, for the trigger-happy gunners of the American landing-craft were unfamiliar with European aircraft, and unable to tell ours from the Germans. So many of our fighters were shot down by the men they were trying to protect that for a time our own fighters were pulled right out of the beach-head area.

The night that the second Mulberry, the artifical harbour, broke up became legendary. For it let go at the height of a really disastrous gale, and the great "bombardons", or steel tanks which were coupled together to make part of the floating roadway, came driving down on us where we lay anchored in the lee. What a wild night ensued! There were the most frightful crashes and grindings as the big tanks crashed into anchored ships, and gunfire all over the place, as ships attempted to sink the units before they were themselves bashed into. Eventually we were ordered to weigh and pursue each individual tank, sinking every one we could round up, charging along through anchored ships in driving rain and howling wind, with guns blazing all about us.

There was the day we lay alongside one of the ships destined to be sunk to form the outer breakwater around the Mulberry harbour at Arromanches. All the British ships used for blockships were stripped-out hulks, but this American vessel had everything aboard, just as the crew had left her. When we wondered at the waste of so much fine new material, the watchman told us that in the time, and at the cost, of stripping and sending home all the material, half a dozen ships could be built back in the States. We believed him, and were glad of the dozens of steaks from her freezer and some of the fine navigational gear from her charthouse.

Like everyone else, we were awed by the fantastic size and shape of all sorts of things being towed past us by fleets of tugs; "Winnie's Wonders", as they were called, included huge concrete caissons, like sea-going grain elevators, to form part of the Mulberry harbours, and gigantic drums, like giant spools of thread, unwinding a plastic pipeline as they were towed towards the beaches by tugs in Operation Pluto (Pipe Line Under The Ocean). Soon we were pumping fuel for vehicles in Normandy all the way from England, via underwater pipeline.

The weeks following the initial D-Day assault were filled with varied action. As the armies crunched inland, we swept ahead of the assaults to open up the new ports of Morlaix and Roscoff. There we passed close to the burned-out hulk of a German destroyer, driven high and dry on the rocks by our own Tribal destroyers *Haida* and *Athabaskan*; an action which had cost the latter's life. Lying on his back in the water, *Athabaskan*'s gallant captain, Johnny Stubbs, had watched the dawning day which would spell death for *Haida* if she lingered longer to pick up the remainder of the survivors still in the water. "Get out of it, *Haida*," he had shouted to her bridge, and *Haida* had been forced to do just that, leaving further rescue work to the German vessels already putting out from shore. John Stubbs, who had led us in the Atlantic in *Assiniboine* and who had welcomed our flotilla so warmly when we arrived in Plymouth, was lost with 128 of his crew, and for us the rusting German hulk, high on the rocks of the Ile de Bas, had special significance.

Earlier, we had swept ahead of the force that landed at Cherbourg, after *Rodney* had softened up the coastal batteries with a tremendous curtain of fire. The shattered concrete fragments of the great fort on the outer mole were vivid testimony to the power of her huge guns.

In the early days of the invasion, the waters off the beaches were filled with every imaginable sort of flotsam, including men alive (head up) and dead (bottom up). We picked up the crew of a Liberator early one morning; as we came alongside their rubber raft the flight lieutenant in charge said "Good morning" to us as casually as a man waiting for a bus. They had been investigating a radar contact the night before—probably from one of the many rocks hereabouts— and, flying low over the water, had switched on their Leigh light, a great floodlight of incredible brilliance. In the sudden glare, the pilot had lost sight of the sea surface, and, misjudging his height, had flown his big Liberator right into the sea. Strangely, the only casualty had been the tail-gunner; everyone else had made it clear as the plane sank, although there was a sprinkling of broken legs and arms.

For all of us in the Channel these were momentous and memorable days. The support groups hunting down U-boats, the Tribals raiding across to the French coast everynight, returning next morning wreathed in glory and heavy with dead, the MGB's and MTB's on their nocturnal forays, as well as we flotilla types messing about the coastal minefields—all of us shared a sense of destiny. We felt ourselves to be participating in the freeing of a continent, of being part of a great crusade that would bring to an end this long struggle against an odious tyranny. It was this euphoria which was to nearly bring about our downfall.

For we had received a signal while we lay in Cherbourg:

Minas was to return to Canada to refit, forthwith. Within five minutes the anchor cable was rattling home and we were on our way.

It was then that I made the mistake which nearly cost us our ship and our lives. I was so intent on getting to Plymouth with all dispatch that I laid off our course to pass from port to port direct, instead of taking the safe dog-leg prescribed in order to pass out of gun range of the island of Alderney, where the Germans had a battery of heavy coast artillery. The direct route would cut off a hour, and would take us seven miles off Alderney, safe enough, surely, for a small ship. We had passed the island before at closer ranges without drawing a shot.

We cleared the Cherbourg approaches, and I went down for breakfast.

Bam!

The shattering explosion brought me to the wardroom door, napkin in hand; a towering waterspout was disappearing, close to our starboard quarter. I raced for the bridge, and for the next quarter-hour we played tag with the shore battery firing at us. The gunners were dead on for range, and only slightly off in deflection; I kept altering course toward the last fall of shot and then the gunners would miss on the opposite side, but it was only a matter of time before they fired two rounds with unchanged deflection.

Desperately, we called the engine room to make smoke; normally, we cranked out clouds of it, but this time, when we needed it, not a smudge.

Finally, a desperate quarterdeck party managed to get a smoke-float over and we tucked gratefully behind its comforting shroud. We put over another smoke-float, just as the bridge window beside me starred and broke, pierced by a bit of shrapnel from the shell bursting alongside. An array of tiny holes suddenly appeared in our funnel, and my heart sank.

But as we moved behind the smoke, the gunners' accuracy fell off markedly. Suddenly, a new hazard appeared: we were running into a minefield, the navigator informed me, and we would have to alter back into clear visibility if we were not to be in the middle of it. Better to risk the shellfire than the certainty of blowing up on a mine; we altered back into the bright sunshine out of the safety of the smoke, and I stared at the distant battery with my glasses. I could see it clearly, the low gunpits topped by a huge, skull-like concrete dome, which must be the observation and control position. That great tower on its forbidding cliff was to haunt my dreams for years; long afterward, I was to return and seek it out, to find it still as formidable and sinister in its peacetime decrepitude as it had seemed before its teeth had been drawn.

Fortunately for all concerned, its gunners had decided against wasting any more ammunition on a now-distant ship; we legged it for Plymouth, home, and mother. For us, the great Channel battle was over.

12
THE GRAVEYARD
OF THE ELEPHANTS

As the Allied armies drove steadily through France toward the German border, the war at sea entered its latest and, as it proved, final phase. Equipped with the schnorkel, a long, pipe-like extension which could be raised above the surface allowing a submerged submarine to run her diesel engines, swarms of U-boats were concentrated in the Irish Sea, the Bay of Biscay, and the western Channel, through which the Allies had to transport all their vital supplies for the armies in Normandy. A large number of Canadian corvettes, including mine, were hustled across to beef up local escorts of convoys in the threatened areas, while British and Canadian support groups prowled about the Channel approaches.

The schnorkel, fitted with valves to keep out water from wavetops while admitting vital air, meant that U-boats were no longer forced to surface to re-charge the batteries that drove their electric motors underwater, and hence were no longer so vulnerable to attack by radar-fitted aircraft. Now they became true submersibles, and instead of attacking in packs on the surface, at night, as before, they lay in wait at periscope depth and attacked, submerged, principally by day.

In any sort of chop, it was extremely difficult to spot the few feet of periscope which appeared at brief intervals above the surface.

The last stages of the Battle of the Atlantic, like the first, were to be fought out on the British doorstep. I was glad to be back in corvettes after a crack at minesweeping, for I had left *Minas* at her refit port and taken command of the veteran corvette *Camrose*. But I was happier still to be back in the civilized conditions of the narrow seas, where voyages

were shorter, weather was better, and assistance of every kind
was more readily available than in the far reaches of the Atlantic. And yet, for all that, this new kind of submarine warfare was a particularly frustrating one for the escorts. We lost
ships, in ones and twos, but seldom had the satisfaction of
making a clean kill. In the shallow Channel waters, a U-boat
would lie motionless on the bottom after making her attack,
while we would go probing around with our asdic and even
our echo-sounder, trying to make out which bump on the
bottom could be a U-boat. What complicated matters, apart
from tidal rips and other submerged distractions, was that the
bottom of the Channel and its approaches was simply carpet-
ed with wrecks, literally thousands of them, for ships had
been sinking there since the dawn of history and had continued to do so right up to the present. The wreck chart, on
which the position of every known wreck was plotted, became a key part of our operating equipment, but in case of
doubt we generally attacked a good contact on the bottom
just to be sure; U-boats had a way of cosying up to a known
wreck to shelter in its immunity. As a result, we occasionally
brought up some strange bits and pieces from ships which
had been lying on the bottom for years; a fragment of a
Tudor warship, perhaps, black as coal, or some of the cabin
fittings from a vessel sunk by the Kaiser's U-boats in the First
World War.

Fog became another bothersome factor; there seemed to be
no end to it in the spring of 1945. We once found ourselves
attempting to pass orders to our little fogged-in Irish Sea convoy by Morse on our siren, for although still a lieutenant
like everyone else in corvettes, I was getting so long in the
tooth as to find myself sometimes senior officer in escorting
these little coastal convoys. We were attempting to button our
Irish Sea section onto the Channel convoy which we'd encountered crossing our bows; in the thick fog, only we escorts
could tell, by our radar, where the other ships were. The
process of signalling a new, safe course to our lot, hidden in
swirling clouds of thick fog, by means of our snuffling,
screeching siren, was guaranteed to put a few more silver
threads among the gold.

Crossing the Bay of Biscay with a big convoy one sunny
midday, there was a tremendous bang and the leading wing
ship nearest to us went up in a pillar of fire. She was a
tanker, heavily loaded with fuel oil, and she burned like a

torch, brighter than the bright sunlight, and covered the sky above with a pall of black smoke. We closed her instantly while the rest of the convoy steamed past and the escort group carried out its proper evolution, each escort searching out its sector. As always, the sight and sound of the burning tanker was appalling; it was the roar, even more than the heat or brightness of the flames, which seemed so daunting. She had been torpedoed in the stern, and as she gradually filled, her bows rose steadily, until they were well clear of the water. She hung there, bows upthrust, in a towering inferno of smoke and flame, while her survivors paddled frantically away in the few rafts and floats they'd managed to get overside.

As we ran in we got a firm asdic contact on a target only a few hundred yards past the doomed ship. It came in, loud and clear, with sharp cut-offs and good definition, moving very slowly left to right, and so hard and clear that the echo on the bridge speakers could be heard all over the ship. In such a position, such an echo could only come from one thing: at last, in this shifting, elusive Channel war, we'd gotten our teeth well into a U-boat!

For us, it was a perfect situation. The convoy was by now well clear, the weather was fine, our set was operating sweetly, and our asdic team, honed to a fine edge by endless drills and a week-long intensive course at the asdic centre in Campbelltown, was eager for blood. We reduced speed and prepared to carry out a textbook attack on this rash U-boat, using our hedgehog. This was a sort of many-barrelled mortar, mounted on our fo'c'sle, which threw a pattern of heavy bombs ahead of the ship. They sank rapidly, and would explode only on contact with the U-boat, or the bottom. An explosion meant a hit, and a hit meant a sinking.

We carried out the prettiest attack we'd ever done; at precisely the right instant, our hedgehog fired, sending its rockets rippling off to fall in a perfect circle, far ahead. In a silence so intense as to be tangible, we held our breaths and listened.

Bang! Bang!

Two hits! We'd done it! We almost burst with exultation; down in the waist the depth-charge crews pounded one another on the back, and from the engine room the Chief called up excitedly to ask if "we'd got the bastard". We had, we had indeed, we assured him, and slowed down still further, as our asdic operator warned us of breaking-up noises just ahead.

And there! Bobbing up fine on the port bow, some large

object surfaced. Wild with excitement, we fixed it with our binoculars, but could make nothing of it. Now there came oil, and we were sure of our kill. But—what was all that? Suddenly, the sea about us seemed to erupt with floating debris. But it was not the splintered wreckage, the little bits of panelling and nondescript domestic flotsam, expected from a sunken U-boat; rather, it was great rectangular-shaped packages of some sort.

Coming close to one, we inspected it minutely; scores of heads craned overside at the strange apparition from the depths. It was a bale of some sort, baled rubber, by George! We were steaming through a sea covered by floating bales of rubber. But it was not until the commodore's signal, reporting not one but two ships torpedoed, that it became clear to us what had happened. Directly behind the torpedoed tanker, a second ship had been hit, and had sunk almost immediately, screened from us by the burning tanker. We had actually picked up her sinking hull, submerged but not yet on the bottom, on our asdic, her twisting motion and increasing depth giving all the effects of a slow-moving submarine. Our attack had been letter-perfect, and the explosion of the hedgehog bombs had broken loose her deck-cargo of baled rubber.

It was a freak occurrence, and a bitter disappointment to us, but it also marked an event of some significance. For although we could not know it at the time, it was to be the last loss, the last U-boat attack, we would sustain; the long attrition of the U-boat war was nearing its end. We were in Portland when the war with Germany ended, and duly celebrated by splicing the mainbrace with a lot of rum for each man, and we were back in Plymouth in time to see the U-boat which had given us so much trouble only days before steer meekly up the Sound, under heavy escort, with her large black flag of surrender flying. But the Channel held one last surprise; for a few days more, convoys still proceeded under escort, and while we were shepherding a Channel section past the Lizard one morning there was a great explosion astern of the rear ship of the outer column, and a fountain of water erupting out of the sea. Instantly, of course, we suspected a torpedo exploding at the end of its run, or possibly an acoustic torpedo inadvertently detonating in the turbulence of the convoy's wake, and we carried out a thorough search after reporting the incident to C.-in-C. Plymouth. We could find no contact, nor could the wing escorts, but in no time at all EG 2, Walker's old group and the cream of the support force crop, came galloping over the horizon, and eagerly sought all relevant details from us. They were hoping, of course, for a lone-wolf U-boat unwilling to surrender and taking one last crack at the hated Allies, and the group longed to tack just one more hide on their barn door. They immediately settled down to comb the waters thoroughly, but they came up empty-handed. The explosion might well have been the detonation of a mine, but we chose to put it down to that category of unexplained detonations described by the late Captain Walker himself as an "ichthyological gefuffle". It allowed us to end our war with a bang.

The whimper was to come later. Summoned into the presence one morning, we were greeted by "Father", as everyone called our aged, delightful Captain D, with his usual: "Morning, *Camrose*; job of work for you this morning."

It was a most unusual assignment; taking the corvette *Lunenburg* under our wing, we were to hop around all the Channel Islands, which had been by-passed by the Allied drive and had only now surrendered, gather up the German men-o'-war which had accumulated there, run them down the Brittany coast to the naval port of l'Orient "and turn them over to the Frogs".

It was a fascinating performance; Woody Thomson of Lunenburg and I went ashore in each of the little island harbours—St. Helier, St. Peterport, St. Anne—and were met by the mayor and a deputation of authorities, who in turn introduced us to the German commanding officers. It was all most awkward; how, after all, did one behave to the vanquished enemy on their home ground, so to speak? Complicating matters was the disparity in strength; during the months following the invasion, all sorts of German craft had sought refuge here, as the other Channel ports fell to the Allied armies. How were two small corvettes to enforce their wishes on dozens of heavily armed destroyers, minesweepers, flak ships, and other odds and ends? Even the armed tug could have blown us both out of the water if he had wanted to make a break for South America.

In the event, everything went swimmingly. We brought our QR2, our senior gunnery rating, with us, equipped with a couple of large gunnysacks. We removed the breech-block firing mechanism from each German gun, popped it in the bag, and suddenly we were dealing with a fleet of unarmed ships. The German officers proved to be embarrassingly subservient. Their fawning, apologetic manner we found enormously disappointing, somehow; we expected resignation, perhaps defiance, from an enemy who had fought so long and so bravely; this smiling servility stuck in our throats. Perhaps it was true that the best of the German navy went into the U-boats.

We put a signalman aboard as many of the Germans as we could staff, and made sure that on these ships there was someone who could translate English into German; these ships we made section leaders, with the remaining ships of that section under their orders.

We then set off for the French port to the south and west of us, our Germans strung out in a long line-ahead formation, with the tug and assorted trawlers bringing up the rear, and Woody cavorting on one flank and us on the other. We shepherded our little flock, a gaggle of ugly ducklings if there ever was one, around the corner and into the approaches of l'Orient, where we turned them, and our bags of breechblocks, over to a French naval escort. What was to become of them we had no idea, but we suspected that for the next year or two the minesweepers would be busy tidying up all the enormous minefields they had been so industriously laying off the French coast for so long. Our operation was over; it had been pure comic opera, from start to finish.

Perhaps appropriately, it was our last "job of work" for Captain D; we got our orders to sail for Canada, and all about us the world of Western Approaches we had known for so long was tumbling about our ears.

The whole command was being run down; its bases were being closed, its ships released to other commands, and its men were queuing up for demobilization. Leave-taking at Londonderry was like a wake; one hardly knew whether to laugh or to cry. We crossed the Atlantic for the last time, with all our lights blazing; the first—and last—time we did so.

We bade Newfyjohn a last, long farewell; already its South Side jetties seemed forlorn, for the mid-ocean types had already taken their departure, and there were few familiar faces left around. We fuelled and backed off into that crowded little harbour for the last time, the three blasts of our siren echoing off the bare hills we had known so well. We took our last look at the pleasant little jerry-built wooden city we had come to love, and where we had made so many friends; in the late afternoon sunshine, the homely buildings glowed warmly, and there seemed not one that did not have some meaning and significance to each of us. We could even make out the rickety staircase leading to the Crowsnest, scene of so many happy hours. It was with a heavy heart that we took old *Camrose* down the harbour she had known so long and so well, cleared the entrance, and stood out past Cape Spear's storm-battered light. In the gathering darkness of early evening, we took our departure for the last time from Cape Race, its great light flicking like a finger in the northern sky, and headed for Halifax and the inevitable end that awaited us there.

Halifax had taken on a special meaning for us since the disgraceful riots that had disfigured VE day. The news of the drunken debauch which had gone on for days had made us ashamed of our service; once again, it seemed to us, the shore navy, the barracks idlers and incompetent officers and the whole ramshackle edifice of Slackers, had made outcasts of seagoing men, blackening the name of the navy and distorting our reputation. We looked on it as a place to get our discharge as quickly as we could.

We passed through the boom defence, steamed up-harbour past George Island, the ferries, the big-ship wharves, and berthed alongside Jetty Four in the dockyard. *Camrose* was home from the wars at last; home to stay. She was never to sail again as an operational ship.

Yet she was not to die all at once. We landed our crew, and most of our officers and men made their farewells and went off to home and civvy street; a handful of us remained to take our ship on her last journey. We moved her across the harbour, first, where working parties from the shore removed her ammunition and depth-charges, her asdic and other technical equipment, and specialized fighting gear of every kind. When they had done and had gone their way, we raised steam and took her away on her last voyage. We cleared the boom at Halifax with never a backward look, and settled into the unaccustomed routine of steaming a ship, in peacetime, from port to port, with no worries or concerns of any kind save the routine ones of simple pilotage.

Sydney in Cape Breton was our first stop; we went alongside the great cranes there and had our Oerlikons and our four-inch mounting, our surface main armament, lifted out of the ship. Poor old *Camrose*; for the first time she showed her years, a veritable toothless tiger; it was surprising what a difference the removal of her forward gun made in her appearance. We hoisted our long de-commissioning pendant; *Camrose* was ready for her last voyage.

It was a sad business; that evening, the last before we were to sail on the first leg of this dismal trip to the boneyard, we pooled the dwindling resources of our wardroom with that of the corvette alongside and set off, in the ship's whaler, for a final party together.

In the twilight of a pleasant summer evening, we picnicked on a point of land not far from the dockyard. We had a pleasant, reminiscent time, a very quiet affair save for a few rousing songs of one sort or another. Towards the end of the proceedings, a cow joined us; it loomed out of the darkness and shouldered into our circle, where it was made much of by one and all and, in lieu of anything better, was offered a cigar, which it declined. Somebody bet our chief engineer, who was from Kenora in western Ontario, that he couldn't ride the cow for more than ten seconds. (To benighted Torontonians anyone from west of the Humber is a cowboy, born and bred.) The chief could not refuse; standing up, he acknowledged the applause with a graceful gesture and moved towards the cow, now fallen into a light doze. Stroking its neck placatingly, he essayed to vault onto its back, which, since he was built on the general lines of a chesterfield, was no easy task. In the event, it proved to be beyond him; the cow, sensing dirty work afoot, gave a heave, shouldered the chief to one side, and disappeared into the night whence it had come, snorting with indignation.

Since, as the chief pointed out, he had never actually been aboard the cow, his ability, once on, to remain seated for the requisite ten seconds had never been put to the test, and it was conceded that all bets were off; we were regaled instead by the fine baritone voice of Number One.

Shortly thereafter, we returned to our virtuous beds and slept the sleep of the just.

Next morning there was a tremendous flap. I was summoned into the office of some four-ringed captain and given the most scathing tongue-lashing; his cow, he maintained, had clocked in that morning too upset to give of its milk in its usual generous manner. His cow, he claimed, had been interfered with and he intended to have the heart's blood of the skunk who had laid a hand on her. If it had been his daughter, his wrath could not have been greater. We were not to be allowed to sail, he told me, until I had given him the name of the man responsible.

I could simply not comprehend the man's fury about a cow which he obviously was pasturing on navy land at navy expense to furnish him with a little fresh milk for his private use; the kind of petty swindle which shore officers seemed to regard as one of the "perks" of office. Yet this pink-faced little bleeder, now throwing a tantrum about his ruddy cow, was of the same rank as Vian when he led his destroyers against *Bismarck,* of Mainguy when he built the mid-ocean groups at Newfyjohn, of Nelson when he interposed his ship against the Spanish line at Cape St. Vincent.

My disbelief must have showed, because he now became utterly fatuous, with threats about "ruining the careers of those responsible". Since the careers referred to could be timed in hours, there was little to worry about, but I was not about to cause concern to one of the corvette's navy's finest engineers at the end of years of hard and distinguished service. I told this incredible man that as the senior officer present I was responsible for any misconduct at last night's affair, and assured him that there had been none. I told him exactly what had happened, save for the names, and reaffirmed that no injury had been done the cow, who had left our midst admired by all.

The captain, calming down somewhat, asked for a formal written report from me, together with the name of the officer responsible, before we would receive sailing orders. I went back to the ship, typed my report, omitted any names but appended an apology for any emotional upset caused the cow by what had been a foolish prank.

In the end, of course, cooler heads prevailed; we received our sailing orders after a few hours' delay, and left with sighs of relief. All the same, it had been a disquieting reminder of the transition we would have to make between the world of the operational navy, where the issues were life and death, and that of the shoreside navy we were coming back to, obsessed with the most trifling concerns and motivated by a pettiness and selfishness completely alien to the way of life of men living literally in the same boat. The end of the war meant the end not only of the corvette navy but of a whole way of life, and we felt an inward qualm as the nature of the world we were returning to, and in which we must now make our way, was brought home to us.

It was a strange trip we made, through the Gulf and up the great stream of the St. Lawrence, in a mood compounded equally of exultation at our pending return to home and family and all the comforts of peace, and of sadness for what we were leaving behind, and above all, for the approaching end of our ship. One by one, the lights and landmarks made familiar to us years before, in trooping trips to Labrador, passed by: Cape Chat, Matane, Father Point. In the calm waters of the river, we decided to let the old girl show what she could really do. For years, even in the heat of action, the Chief, like all engineers, never let his beloved engines run to their utter limit; always, like any prudent man, he kept a little something in reserve. He had nursed his engines, his boilers, all through the war years; now, at the end of their career, he assented to a full-speed trial. We fixed our position carefully, and laid out a precisely measured course on our chart; then we rang down for full speed, a triple ring, and held onto our hats...

Freed of her heavy burden of guns and depth-charges and extra fuel, of men and supplies of every kind, old *Camrose* fairly flew. With a great bow-wave flaring out on each side like wings, she tore through the water, her wake a ribbon of boiling foam astern. As the Chief and his delighted crew in stokehold and engine room cranked her up and opened all the taps to their fullest extent, a shimmering haze hung over her funnel-top, and everything in the ship shook with the vibrations of her surging propeller. The shore marks fairly whizzed by; as we neared the transit that marked the end of our allotted course, the navigator stood ready with his stopwatch. Click! We had done it; the vibration eased as the revolutions dropped, while cheering came faintly up the engine-room voice-pipes.

A little calculation produced the startling result: *Camrose*, in the last hours of her life, had gone faster than ever before; the 18.2 knots she had just chalked up exceeded even her highest speed achieved on her acceptance trials, when she was fresh from the builder's yard. We all gave her a cheer for that, and wondered what was to become of her.

We were bound for Sorel, roughly halfway up the St. Lawrence between Quebec City and Montreal, where we were to hand her over to officials of War Assets Corporation for disposal. Most of the ships, we knew, were destined to be scrapped, but some at least, we had heard, were being bought up by nations in South America and elsewhere for further service in their navies. Built and launched in 1941, *Camrose* was relatively old as corvettes went; probably the ships chosen for further naval service would be selected from the more recent productions. Nevertheless, our ship was in excellent shape, and there was always the chance that her smart appearance might just tip the scales in her favour. Taking advantage of our sunny summer weather, we turned to with paint and brush, all of us, officers and men, and touched up her paintwork where the removal of wiring and instruments had left bare patches on her bridge, in her wireless and radar cabins. Always well-kept, she needed only a touch or two here and there, and a good scrubbing of decks and messdecks; she arrived at Sorel gleaming and immaculate, inside and out, her teak decks fore and aft as bright as a yacht's, her brightwork polished and her bulkheads and corticene spotless. We had done for her everything we could; her fate now lay with others, and we led her in to her graveyard bedecked in her finest, like some sacrificial maiden led to the fatal altar.

Off Sorel, we picked up our pilot, a voluble little French-Canadian chap, who guided us, with a torrent of orders and cautions and gestures through a channel into a cluster of reedy islands, among which we picked our way before emerging at our final destination.

Ahead of us, a long stretch of water opened up, hemmed in by a featureless line of low, swampy sandbars. And in that stretch, moored head to tail at rows of buoys, lay the entire corvette navy, together with the destroyers and frigates that had led the escort groups. There were hundreds of them, still in sea-worn Western Approaches camouflage, but strangely altered. For one thing they had no guns; for another, there was not a sign of life. They were no longer ships, but mere lifeless hulks, the bare bones of once-great fighting ships, lying huddled in decaying ranks in this dismal place. We had arrived at the graveyard of the elephants.

As we edged to our allotted place alongside a dead corvette, we gazed about in wonder, in awe, in real horror. It seemed a terrible thing, somehow, to reduce this mighty force, which only weeks before had won command of the bitter North Atlantic, to so many rusting hulks.

The sight of so many veteran ships, built at such effort and cost and fought with such hardihood and endurance, lying forgotten in this ghastly backwater was, literally, a terrible sight; nobody who saw it will ever forget it. It was the Battle of the Atlantic reduced to a few hundred thousand tons of rusting metal, and it sobered us as nothing else could.

After this numbing spectacle, all was anti-climax. A fellow in a fedora hat came aboard, knocked back the last of my precious Maderia like so much soda-pop, and wrote me out a little receipt for *Camrose*: "received from the Department of Naval Defence, the corvette *Camrose*, together with . . ." etc. etc. It was a slip of paper, the kind one would expect when a used lawnmower changes hands.

Towards sunset, the ship began to die. The last of the steaming party supplies were embarked, along with most of our crew, in a big motorboat; we had gathered, all of us, a few minutes earlier to splice the mainbrace for the last time. We'd mixed everything potable in the ship—a little rum, some sherry, half a bottle of crème de menthe—and measured it out to each man. We'd toasted the King, of course, and then our coxswain, a grizzled, taciturn old veteran who'd been with the ship since commissioning, stepped forward to make the toast we were gathered for. "To *Camrose*, a great ship!" he said, and we all drank to her for the last time.

Down below now, the Chief had shut off all steam; the exhaust fans, which throbbed aboard day and night, at sea and alongside, stopped, and the silence was so sudden it made us jump. For steam was the lifeblood of the ship, and when it ceased to flow, *Camrose* ceased to live.

We had only a few minutes to wait before the boat arrived to take the last of us ashore. I went up to the bridge, and leaned on the binnacle and looked out at the grisly scene, lit now by the glow of a dying sunset. There was *Assinibone*, the old "Bones" of our early group, and alongside was *Trail*, the corvette in which I had spent two eventful years, and about her were all the ships we had sailed with, in one group or another, for what seemed all our adult life. Each one brought memories, evoked faces—*Morden* there had once startled everyone by bringing in a record ninety-four survivors, many of them women and children, and there was *Moose Jaw*, famous in the fleet for her wardroom Moosemilk. Here was *Port Arthur*, Ted Simmons' old warhorse, and "Sally Rand", the *St. Laurent*, which had made such a name for herself in the Western Approaches. And there was Cowboy Jackson's old bucket, and *Dauphin*, a chummy ship from refit days.

All dead now; not only dead but forgotten. Seagulls perched on the dodger where George Hall, my old captain, once leaned; the rasping screech of a rusty fitting as the ship moved to a slight swell only emphasized the silence of death all around us.

I took a last long look around at those lifeless ships, haunted by so many ghosts, then closed the cover of the voice-pipe to the wheelhouse, severing the umbilical cord which had bound me to *Camrose* for so long. For *Camrose*, which had sunk U757 and shot down two bombers, which had screened the invasions of Sicily and Normandy, which had fought off U-boat packs in a dozen fierce encounters and had helped bring innumerable merchant ships safely to port, this great ship of ours, was dead now, and I must leave her here among the bones of her sisters.

I turned and ran down the ladder, and into the waiting boat. And I left behind me a ship and a fleet, a host of friends and a way of life that I would never see again. The corvette navy was dead, and I walked away into the strange civilian world of peace.

13
I REMEMBER,
I REMEMBER . . .

We have stood, in the unaccustomed attitude of parade "attention", at more than a score of Remembrance Day ceremonies now, in various parts of Canada. Sometimes it has been cold and blustery, sometimes chill and bright, but the way we remember it is in the rain, when the bugler sounds the Last Post and we are left alone with our memories. Around us are the few from the Old War, with their dreadful memories of blood and mud at Passchendaele or Vimy, Hill 60, Ypres or Amiens. Our own thoughts are of another, newer, war—yet a war which already seems part of a dim past.

It is not the dark memories which come to us now: the terror of ships afire in a black night, of crashing seas in an Iceland gale, of the white-faced crewmen of the destroyer *Ottawa*, the smell of death already upon them; of the shredded, bloated horrors, floating under clouds of seagulls, in the dawn-grey seas after a convoy attack. Years of peacetime pursuits, of family life and television and business pressures, have eased these memories from our conscious mind; it is only in dreams that they live on now.

On Remembrance Day our memories are of a different kind. We remember when the world was an exciting place in which to be young and when, with a thousand others, we were likely to be sent halfway around the earth and back again, without a care for tomorrow. One had a sense of destiny in those days; of being a part of historic events, of helping to mould a new and better world. How innocent, how naive, how pathetic it all seems now!

But we remember only the pleasant times, the high-spirited

times. We remember Tiger Turner standing on his head in the punchbowl at Captain D's cocktail party, and the midnight discussions of the works of Shaw and Chesterton with Tommy Holland over cocoa in a deserted middle-watch wardroom, tossed in a raging sea. We remember the sudden serenity of Lough Foyle, the luxury of fresh linen that went with the end of yet another eastward crossing, and the gay signals to the wrennery at Boom Hall as the escort group filed upriver to Londonderry. We remember warm and happy hours at the Crowsnest in Newfyjohn; aboard the mother ships *Baldur* and *Vulcan* in Iceland's Hvalfjord; in the brass-bound murkiness of the Shakespearean Cellar in Londonderry. Happy, light-hearted times; the happier for their stark and fateful background. One cherishes the few sunlit days all the more in seasons of rain and despair.

They are all gone now: Holland and Millthorpe, Harvey and the rest of them, in the shattered wrecks of ships scattered across the wide ocean floor. We who are left, are young no more; the eager boys' faces of yesterday are creased by time and pouched with civilian living. Yet still, across the widening gulf that yawns between that age and the present, the memory of our shared youth brings a pang to our heart, and moisture to our eyes.

It is not for the dead that we mourn, those bright hearts we have been revisiting in memory. Rather it is for the passing of our lost youth, and for the spirit of adventure and high endeavour which passed with it.

GLOSSARY

~~~~~~

Abaft behind, relative to something aboard ship.

Aft, after towards the stern.

Asdic submarine detection gear based on sub-sonic transmission. Later, the U.S. term "sonar" was adopted.

Astern behind, relative to a ship.

Bollard vertical post around which ropes are secured.

Boom defence underwater steel netting, supported by buoys and fitted with a gate, stretched across harbour to keep out submarines.

Boom defence vessels located either side of gate to open and close it as required.

Bosun or *boatswain* senior rating in charge of upper deck.

Bosun's mate messenger who carries or promulgates messages.

Bosun's pipe shrill whistle carried by bosun's mate.

Bow front end of ship or boat.

Breastline warp at right angles to ship's centre-line, used to hold ship close alongside.

Bridge elevated platform from which ship is conned.

Caisson a concrete tank which can be sunk in designated place by admitting water through valves; used for floating harbour.

Carley float lifesaving device with slat floor suspended inside a floating ring.

Coxswain senior petty officer in the ship, who takes wheel for all important manoeuvres. Responsible for discipline in small ships.

Dan buoy float fitted with anchor and pole topmark.

178

Davit post at shipside used to raise or lower boat, and other objects.

Dodger wood or canvas screen sheltering bridge from weather.

Dog-watch two two-hour watches—4-6 p.m. and 6-8 p.m.

Drogue canvas funnel dragged through air or water.

Flag officer senior officer above rank of captain; flies rank flag.

Flotilla organized grouping of destroyers or smaller ships.

Fo'c'sle, forecastle forward part of ship. In a corvette, it houses most of the crew.

Funnel ship's smokestack.

Gunner gunnery specialist, usually warrant officer.

Gunner's mate petty officer gunnery specialist, navy's drill sergeant.

Guns used as title for officer in charge of gunnery department.

Halyard light rope used to hoist flags to mast or yard.

HSD (Higher Submarine Detection) the senior asdic rating in the ship.

Lee downwind side; in the shelter of downwind side.

Leeward downwind, away from the wind.

Leigh light light of intense brilliance, used by aircraft in night operations.

Main deck the principal overall deck.

MGB motor gunboat.

MTB motor torpedo boat.

Navel pipes tubes carrying anchor cables from upper decks to chain locker.

Oerlikon light rapid-firing cannon firing variety of shell.

Pom-pom single or multi-barrelled gun firing 2-lb. shell.

Pusser naval slang for proper, official, or regulation style.

Quarter diagonally astern and out to one side of ship.

Salvoes system of firing guns by direct order, applying corrections as required to bring fall of shot on target.

Signalman rating who transmits messages by light, flag, semaphore.

Singling up to reduce warps ashore to one of each.

Snotty midshipman, most junior officer rank. So called because three buttons on cuff were traditionally intended to prevent him wiping nose on sleeve.

Stanchion vertical metal support for rail or lifeline.

Star shell   fired from gun, it releases flare suspended from parachute.

Stern   back end of ship or boat.

Subbie   sublieutenant, senior to midshipman, junior to lieutenant.

Trot-buoys or trots   midstream buoys used to moor ships fore and aft.

Waist   midship section of upper deck.

Warp   rope used to secure ship to shore.

Whaler   double-ended pulling boat, capable of being sailed.

Yard-arm   outer end of a yard crossed on a mast.

ABOUT THE AUTHOR

~~~~~~

James B. Lamb joined the RCNVR in 1939 and spent the war on several corvettes. He commanded two, HMCS *Minas* and HMCS *Camrose*. After the war, Mr. Lamb embarked on a varied career as a newspaper man. His articles have appeared in a wide variety of newspapers and magazines, including *The Toronto Star*, *The Globe Magazine*, *Saturday Night*, *The Saturday Review*, and *The Financil Post*.

Mr. Lamb lives at Big Harbour overlooking the Bras d'Or Lakes.

SIGNET Novels You'll Want to Read

☐ **THE LUCK OF THE IRISH: A Canadian Fable by Harry J. Boyle.** A wild and wondrous novel about a miracle called love . . . "A toothsome story . . . a tale to be savored." —**Hamilton Spectator** (#YE18—$2.25)

☐ **CLOSE TO THE SUN AGAIN by Morley Callaghan.** A great writer's triumphant new novel of a man's final reckoning . . . "Masterful, gripping, powerful . . . Callaghan's best." —**Winnipeg Free Press** (#YE8—$2.50)

☐ **A POPULATION OF ONE by Constance Beresford-Howe.** The exuberantly sexy novel about an unforgettable young woman aching to spread her wings . . . "It rings true!" —**Ottawa Journal** (#YE7—$2.25)

☐ **SANDBARS by Oonah McFee.** A remembrance of things long past—the moving story of a woman's search for herself . . . "Long, luscious, intricate . . . gem-studded all the way!"—**The Canadian** (#YE6—$2.50)

☐ **THE INVENTION OF THE WORLD by Jack Hodgins.** A vividly memorable novel that will take you into a magical world. **The Invention of the World** "rings with needle-sharp authenticity . . . a powerful evocation of life in its unquenchable vitality . . . rich, complex, explosive!"— **Toronto Star** (#YE5—$2.50)

☐ **FARTHING'S FORTUNES by Richard B. Wright.** "All the wonderful elements of picaresque adventure including plenty of vigorous sex . . . a pleasure . . . ONE OF THE BEST CANADIAN NOVELS OF THE YEAR!"—**Vancouver Sun** (#YE4—$2.50)

☐ **CHILD OF THE MORNING by Pauline Gedge.** The fiery epic of the beautiful woman who dared ascend to history's most powerful throne . . . "A marvelous saga . . . a torrent of passion and intrigue!"—**Toronto Star** (#YE3—$2.50)

Other Nonfiction Bestsellers from SIGNET

☐ **TRUDEAU by George Radwanski.** The real man behind the image . . . "The most successful exploration of the man so far!"—**Toronto Globe and Mail.** A Book-of-the-Month Club Main Selection. (#YE17—$2.50)

☐ **MIKE: The Memoirs of the Right Honourable Lester B. Pearson, Volume I.** From minister's son to minister of state—a magnificent human odyssey. "This book makes it clear that the Mike Pearson whom the world came to know and admire is the real Mike Pearson. . . . Mike is full of stories and anecdotes, threaded with the names of the famous people who were his friends and confidants." —**Time** (#J5766—$1.95)

☐ **MIKE: The Memoirs of the Right Honourable Lester B. Pearson, Volume III—1957-1968.** In the climactic volume of his best-selling Memoirs, Lester Pearson tells the story of his difficult, dramatic, but ultimately triumphant years as Prime Minister of Canada. (#J7272—$1.95)

☐ **I CHOSE CANADA: The Memoirs of the Honourable Joseph R. "Joey" Smallwood, Volume I—Light of Day.** The candid, colourful, compelling personal saga of the making of a man and the molding of a leader. (#J6662—$1.95)

☐ **I CHOSE CANADA: The Memoirs of the Honourable Joseph R. "Joey" Smallwood, Volume II—The Premiership.** The years of power and testing—when a colourful, controversial leader fought to turn a dream of progress into a triumphant reality. (#J6663—$1.95)

☐ **TORSO: The Evelyn Dick Case by Marjorie Freeman Campbell.** Canada's most lurid, sensational and suspenseful murder trial, with all its scandals, shocks, and still controversial findings has been re-created—in a fascinating narrative no novelist would dare invent, and no fiction could surpass. "It all comes alive again."—**Hamilton Spectator** (#W6971—$1.50)